ATLAS OF THE BATTERED CHILD SYNDROME

Atlas of the Battered Child Syndrome

J. M. Cameron,
M.D., Ph.D. (Glas.), M.R.C. Path.,
D.M.J. (Path.)
Professor of Forensic Medicine, University of London
At London Hospital Medical College

L. J. Rae,
M.A. (Camb.), M.B. B.Chir., M.R.C.S.
(Eng.), L.R.C.P. (Lond.), D.M.R.E. (Camb.)
Consulting Radiologist, The London Hospital

Foreword by
The Rt. Hon. Lord Justice Lawton

CHURCHILL LIVINGSTONE
EDINBURGH LONDON AND NEW YORK 1975

65688

CHURCHILL LIVINGSTONE
Medical Division of Longman Group Limited

Distributed in the United States of America by Longman Inc.,
New York and by associated companies, branches and
representatives throughout the world

© Longman Group Limited 1975

First published 1975

ISBN 0 443 01253 9

Filmset on 'Monophoto' 600 by Fyldetype Limited, Kirkham, PR4 3BJ, England
Printed in Great Britain

Foreword

During my twenty-five years in practice at the Bar, which
ended in December, 1960, I never once had to
prosecute or defend in a 'baby battering' case; and I
do not remember ever being in Court whilst such a case
was being tried. Such cases of cruelty to children as
did come before the Courts were usually based on neglect
rather than maltreatment. In January, 1961, I was
appointed a Judge of the Queen's Bench Division of
the High Court. At the Leeds Spring Assize in 1961
I tried my first 'baby battering' case; the forensic
pathologist who gave evidence for the Crown was
Professor Polson who was, and still is, one of the leading
experts in this field. Since then I have tried, or been
concerned with in the Court of Appeal, a number of
similar cases.

My judicial experience has, I think, covered the whole
bracket of possibilities. I have had to deal with a brutal
stepfather who found his wife's baby an inconvenience:
he was convicted of murder. In contrast I have had the
case of an immature teenager mother from a secure and
stable background who married an insensitive and
feckless young man with very different social standards
from hers. In between I have had cases of 'drop-out'
parents, psychopathic fathers, mothers suffering from
subnormality and immigrant mothers who found life in
England too much for them.

Why in the past fifteen years have the Courts had to
deal with these cases so frequently when in the decades
before such cases were seldom tried? The post-1945
increase in violent crime seems an unlikely explanation.
There always have been brutal parents. The inference
must be that such cases never came to the notice of the
police. Before the National Health Service started some
of the children may not have had any medical attention.
Family doctors may often have suspected that their
infant patients had been maltreated; but they would
have felt that they had to accept the explanations given
for obvious injuries as there was no way of refuting
them. Further, if a Judge may be allowed to say so, until
the last decade many doctors seem to have had a blind
spot in diagnosis. They seldom asked themselves how a
fall from a cot or a pram could have caused fractures of
the ribs and metaphysial injuries.

The past is behind us. The medical and nursing

professions have been alerted to the 'battered baby'. This has been due in large measure to the publicity given to the subject by the late Professor Francis Camps and to the writings in the professional journals and the research work of Professor Cameron. This book records the results of their work. In clear terms he sets out what doctors examining infants should look for in order to exclude the possibility of maltreatment; and he identifies the tell-tale indications of the use of violence. With this book the family doctor should have no difficulty in deciding when further tests and examinations should be carried out and junior paediatricians, radiologists and forensic pathologists will have a guide to such examinations and tests.

As Professor Cameron shows, doctors are no longer obliged to accept the explanations for injuries given by parents or guadian. Expert examination often reveals that such explanations cannot be true. This is what happened in the case of murder to which I have already referred. The explanation and history given by the stepfather had been accepted by a number of doctors, including one of considerable experience. Professor Cameron's histological experiments demonstrated that the stepfather must have lied.

The final chapter in this book deals with prevention and treatment. These are aspects of the subject which seem the most difficult. I have little confidence in the part the Courts can play in preventing the maltreatment of infants. Knowledge (if there is any) that a brutal father in Newcastle had been sent to prison for five years for ill-treating a baby is unlikely to stop a similar type of father in London from punching a crying baby in the mouth. The deterrent element in punishment can have little, if any, value in this kind of case. The only element which may have any value is that of retribution. The Courts, by the sentences imposed, must show that Society will not tolerate the maltreatment of children. In many of these cases, however, if Society knew the full facts (and the newspapers seldom give them) it would not want punishment to be imposed but help to be given. More good is likely to come from the early detection of the signs of maltreatment than from prosecution.

Cornwall,
January, 1975

Preface

There are still many people—doctors, lawyers and social workers among them—who deny that battering exists at all. It is estimated that almost 5,000 babies and children are attacked by their father, mother or guardian each year and that approximately 15 per cent die. Many cannot bring themselves to accept that 'ordinary' people could ever attack their own children. It was not until the 1950's that American doctors recognised that many such children had definitely been attacked and it was not until 1962 when Professor Kempe used the phrase 'Battered Child Syndrome' that the subject really became widely discussed. Following Professor Kempe's lead social workers all over the world began to look more closely at the children coming to them with puzzling injuries. Although the safety of the child must be the primary consideration one must remember that battering parents need help and above all a good relationship with the helping person; priority in many cases for re-housing, day nursery placement and even temporary reception of the children into care during periods of stress and crises. Co-operation between doctors and social agencies is essential at all stages. Mutual respect for the duties, responsibilities and professional practises of the several disciplines involved in the management of the battered child and his family is an important aspect to the problem, which will be solved only by the achieving of a greater understanding of its underlying causation. If this succeeds there may be less cause for the almost hysterical demand for legislation to introduce obligatory reporting of cases when a child is found to be injured, for accidents can happen.

We have tried to draw attention to the identification of the conditions and tracing them on the radiological findings and differential diagnosis. In addition we have included a chapter on the ophthalmic aspects of the 'Battered Child Syndrome' by our colleague, Mr. Alan Mushin. It is only fairly recently that it has become medically established that there are ophthalmic aspects in the condition, but in the past little attention had been focused on such manifestations, although there had been reports of associated retinal detachment and curious peripheral chorio-retinal atrophy. It is hoped that after reading this textbook doctors, lawyers, social workers and the police will be encouraged to take a deeper interest in the diagnosis, prevention and treatment of the condition, because not one of them can afford to become blasé: after all it was Socrates who said: 'If I am wise, it is only because I know I am ignorant'.

1975

J.M.C.
L.J.R.

Acknowledgements

The authors wish to acknowledge the numerous colleagues who have assisted them and for the cases which they have lent or referred and, in particular the Consultant Paediatricians at The London Hospital and Queen Elizabeth Hospital for Children, Hackney Road, Bethnal Green, London.
The authors are deeply conscious of the radiographic expertise of Miss V. Brodie and the photographic expertise of Mr. R. F. Ruddick and wish to thank them for their conscientious and co-operative assistance.
They are, in addition, particularly grateful to the various Coroners and Chiefs of Constabulary who gave permission for case reference and permission to reproduce various photographs.

Contents

1. Introduction

Child abuse is a major problem for accident and emergency departments, children's hospitals, general practitioners, social workers, the police, and many others concerned with the welfare of children. The injuries seen include, for example, fractures, bruises, lacerations, soft tissue swellings and burns. Subdural effusion, as a result of direct injury to the skull or by vigorous shaking; damage to the liver or perforation of the stomach or intestine; emotional deprivation, starvation, dehydration, anaemia, growth retardation, or poisoning are also recorded. A child may be poisoned by deliberate administration of a drug, by giving an overdose, or by deliberately leaving poisonous material conveniently near him. Most victims of child abuse are under 4 years old and many under 2. How prevalent these serious assaults are is unknown. A general practitioner might on average see a case every five years.

The majority of 'battering parents' are more or less normal parents who are worn out by their small children—parents who are lonely, poorly, immature, or under emotional or financial stress, with no one to turn to for help. The batterer is usually the mother or father, but sometimes a grandparent or other children. If one parent batters the child, the other one almost certainly knows about it and aids and abets (Kempe, 1971).

The diagnosis can be difficult to reach and impossible to prove. There may be a suspicious delay between an injury and the visit to the doctor. The story given may not agree with the physical findings and the explanation of injuries may be vague. The parents may show inappropriate agitation or evidence of rejection, bitterly describing the child's constant crying or his backwardness, which examination fails to confirm. Suspicious features are injuries in different stages of resolution; bruises for which there is no good explanation, especially on the face; bite marks, a torn frenulum linguea; or the child may be distinctly apathetic. If subdural effusion is present, there are almost always retinal haemorrhages. The specialist has to eliminate other diseases, such as coagulation defects in the case of bruising, and a wide variety of conditions if the baby seems merely to be failing to thrive.

1

A working party, the Tunbridge Wells Study Group, under the auspices of the Spastic's Society and with the help of the Department of Health and Social Security has published an excellent report on the problem. It emphasizes that rehabilitation of the family is more important to society than punishment and that battering parents need help and not condemnation. It also brings out the importance of team work between the hospital, family doctor, social services, and police, and condemns precipitate unilateral action. Though doctors dislike the idea of involving the police, fearing they might be breaking their patient's confidence or that police interrogation might result and so make further help impossible, co-operation with the police is strongly advised.

Radiology plays an essential part in the investigation and diagnosis of the Battered Baby Syndrome. By this examination the radiologist should be able to state that not only are certain skeletal injuries caused by child abuse, but that these injuries are caused in a certain way and are of a certain age.

It has been stated by some authorities that a radiograph cannot distinguish between injuries caused by an assault and those resulting from an accident. This may be true of the older child who is mobile and therefore more prone to accidental injuries, but it is certainly not true of the baby who is confined to the cot or pram or who is not yet fully mobile. As the majority of battered babies are in this latter category, the remarks and illustrations in the following text will refer mainly to this age group.

The main diagnostic features are the metaphysial lesions and the multiple rib fractures; injuries that can only be caused by non-accidental trauma, except in cases of bone disease or where the baby is involved in a vehicular accident.

The illustrations have been selected from several hundred cases of proved battered babies. A proportion of the illustrations are radiographs of post-mortem specimens of babies whose deaths have been reported to one of Her Majesty's coroners. It is the custom nowadays to radiograph the whole body prior to autopsy and then to dissect out and re-radiograph any bone that appears to be damaged. In this way the smallest injury is detected in detail and one has thus been able to piece together a comprehensive picture of the type

of skeletal injuries that should be looked for in the live
suspected battered baby where the small injuries may
not be so clearly demonstrated radiographically.
The mechanisms by which these injuries are caused are
dealt with for two reasons; the first is that it helps to
establish or confirm the diagnosis especially where the
history is at variance with the radiographic findings.
The second reason is that where legal proceedings have
been instituted one is liable to be asked to give an
opinion as to how the injuries were caused.
It is to be hoped that this book will prove to be of
some help in establishing the diagnosis, especially to
the casualty officer who may be the first person to
examine the battered baby and upon whose correct
decision the baby's life might depend.

2. General View of the Battered Child Syndrome

It is not easy to give a simple definition of the 'battered child syndrome'. It is a term used to define a clinical condition in young children, usually under three years of age, who have recieved non-accidental, wholly inexcusable violence or injury on one or more occasions, including minimal as well as severe or fatal trauma, for what is often the most trivial provocation, by the hand of an adult in a position of trust, generally a parent, guardian or foster parent. In addition to physical injury, there may be deprivation of nutrition, care and affection in circumstances which indicate that such deprivation is not accidental (Cameron, 1970, 1972, 1974).

The battered baby produces such an emotional reaction of revulsion that it may well be rejected as improbable by both the legal profession, who tend to require a high standard of proof in many cases, and the medical profession.

The term 'battered baby' is so emotive (Cooper, 1970) that perhaps it should be dropped, yet it describes the actual situation very clearly and is useful diagnostically. Other terms that have been suggested include the 'physically abused child', the 'maltreated child' or the 'ill-treated child' syndrome.

The thought that an adult, in a position of trust, could be directly responsible for such an action is so repugnant to natural feeling that it does not come readily to mind. Despite published efforts in the lay and medical press to clarify and to define the legal, medical and social issues associated with the syndrome, some doctors still find it hard to accept the reality of wilful abuse of children. This may be due to an element of lack of confidence in their own judgment, fear that such suspicion would necessitate violating the ethics of their oath of secrecy, or because it may jeopardise their doctor-patient relationship. They may feel that a threat of criminal investigation in any case would increase the danger of other parents not bringing their children to hospital when battered (Cameron, 1970, 1972, 1974). Numerous battered babies are at present simply accepted as accident cases, treated and promptly returned to the possibly fatal hazards of their homes.

4

The cases which come to light are merely the 'tip of the iceberg' (Simpson, 1965).

No-one wants to believe or even think that the ordinary young man or woman one passes in the street could, driven by some terrible impulse, swing their baby by the ankles and bash his head against walls or furniture; shake or jump on his chest until his ribs are crushed, his diaphragm torn or his liver or intestine ruptured; or burn or knock him into unconsciousness, coma and death. According to Kempe (1970), every parent is a potential 'baby basher'. There can be few who, at one time or another, have not been exasperated beyond endurance by the behaviour of their children (Fleming, 1967). Fortunately for most, the expression of their exasperation stops short of real violence. However, there must be a spectrum of violence ranging from corrective trauma from a zealous parent to deliberate cruelty (Cameron, 1970). Parental discipline has consistently alternated between complete abandonment of physical punishment and its excessive use to a point of savagery. Physical punishment for economic gain was common during the period of Industrial Revolution in the United Kingdom as well as elsewhere, with children as young as the under 10 age group frequently chained to industrial manufacturing devices for as long as 12 to 16 hours at a stretch.

Throughout history many children have been neglected or deprived. Others have suffered from physical violence inflicted deliberately as a deterrent, a punishment, an incentive to work or for less understandable reasons. Much cruelty and neglect was accepted as inevitable and even desirable. Society has only recently come to recognize the needs of deprived, exploited and abused children, and statutory and voluntary bodies provide for their welfare, while the law attempts to punish adults for, or deter them from, causing undue suffering.

The battered baby syndrome is a particular facet of the large and complex problem of maltreatment of children. It has sufficiently characterised features to be recognized as a special entity while nevertheless having much in common with other social and medical pathologies associated with parental failure.

In 1946 Caffey drew attention to the apparently increasing frequency of subdural haematoma in infants accompanied by fractures of long bones and he later (1957) offered the possible explanation of parental neglect and abuse as a cause of this association of symptoms. Although other reports (Silverman, 1953; Woolley and Evans, 1955; Altman and Smith, 1960; and Gwinn, Lewin and Paterson, 1961) have referred to this disease of maltreatment as 'unrecognized trauma'; it was Kempe and his associates (1962) who first called it the 'battered child syndrome'. Griffiths and Moyniham (1963) were the first to describe it in the United Kingdom, emphasising the importance of multiple epiphyseal injuries.

When a doctor is called to see an injured child, particularly under the age of three, he must always consider the diagnosis of a battered baby. Nevertheless he should not on the slightest provocation start a 'witch-hunt', for accidents do happen.

No other entity better illustrates the need for a comprehensive approach to the investigation of unnatural death than that of childhood maltreatment, and no other calls for better teamwork. No matter how straightforward the findings may appear initially, or how elaborate and complete the confession (carefully elucidated after all the required precautions), the gathering of all the documentary evidence at the time of the preliminary investigation should proceed according to an orderly pattern. One must assume that the 'confession' may well be 'thrown out' of court or that some subsequent findings in the investigation may well reverse the hypothesis which had been evolved at the initial investigation. The absence of overt trauma on the exterior of the body should in no instance be considered a contraindication for a full clinical examination or, in a dead child, an autopsy, since it often bears no relationship to the trauma on the interior of the body. One should initially inspect the body carefully to note the nature of the clothing, the degree of its cleanliness and the state of repair or disrepair. This should be noted, together with the general external characteristics, including height, weight, state of nutrition (including any suggestion of apparent selective nutritional deficiency). Any discrepancy no matter how subtle, such as disparity between the distribution of the stasis and the alleged terminal position of the body; between the body temperature, and the alleged final care by the parents; or between the obvious state of the nutrition and/or the well being of the infant or child; and the alleged concern of the parents should be carefully followed-up. Photographs, with careful drawings or even tracings, may afford an opportunity to reach a conclusion concerning the nature of the weapon used to inflict such wounds and may be of great help in a subsequent investigation. Each wound should be specifically topographically located on the body with reference to known anatomical landmarks. In cases of autopsy routine histological examination should be carried out on every organ in all cases, particularly the eyes (see Chapter 4).

Recent contributions to the literature point out the importance, in addition, of a general toxicological examination to rule out the introduction of exogenous poisons, or overdoses of therapeutic agents, as contributory factors to the injury or death of these children. The toxicological assay should be qualitative as well as quantitative and as comprehensive as the scope of the toxicological laboratory will allow. This, in part, will depend on the degree of suspicion of the clinician or the pathologist.

No contemporary discussion of child abuse would be complete without commenting on the impact of the drug scene and illicit drug traffic on the next generation of teenagers. Children born into a transient commune type of domestic situation could be more prone to suffer from any form of the patterns of childhood maltreatment. This is not limited to the abandonment, deprivation of food and hygienic amenities, often similarly neglected by the parents, but may include, while the parents are under the influence of certain drugs, sadistic treatment and punishment with long lasting scars or death. Similarly, among those afflicted with habitual addiction, the possibility of a newborn addicted child has been repetitively described within the literature.

Most published work supports the observation of Fontana, Donovan, and Wong (1963) that usually one particular child in a family is selected and becomes the target for abuse and neglect, whereas the other siblings are well cared for and show no evidence of ill-treatment. Of 78 battered children investigated by the National Society of Prevention of Cruelty to Children (Skinner and Castle, 1969), however, it was noted that in families where the first child was battered there was a 13:1 chance that a subsequent child would be injured. Clinicians have a duty and a responsibility to the child to evaluate the problem fully and to guarantee that no repetition of the trauma, either to this child or to any other child, will be permitted to occur. Unfortunately the condition is frequently not recognized or, if diagnosed, is inadequately handled by the clinician because of either hesitation to bring the case to the attention of the proper authorities or the doctor's reluctance to report such a case since it may involve entanglement in legal matters. A major diagnostic feature of this syndrome is the marked discrepancy between the clinical findings and the historical data as supplied by the parents. Because of this there is a reluctance on the part of many clinicians to accept the radiological signs as indicative of repetitive trauma and possible abuse. To the informed clinician the bones tell a story the child is too young or too frightened to tell (Cameron, Johnson and Camps, 1966). There can be little difficulty in differentiation between disease and trauma if proper laboratory and radiological investigations are available, although it must be stressed that trauma may occur to a child which is not healthy. In fact, it may be the ill child whose crying precipitates violence.

The lay press and all forms of mass media in the past two decades have made it abundantly clear that there is virtually no conceivable form of inhumanity to children that has not been documented. Newspaper accounts have described in vivid detail instances of such inhuman acts as holding a child against a radiator, burning him with cigarettes, immersing him in boiling water until extensive burns result (Fig. 2.1) or even prolonged psychological trauma.

CHARACTERISTIC INJURIES

The serious injuries are subdural haemorrhage with or without a fractured skull, and injuries within the abdomen such as a rupture of the liver (Fig. 2.2) or bruising of the intestine. The diagnosis is confused by denial of any accident or explanations by the parent such as the following:

1 He bumped his head against the cot
2 He bruises easily
3 He fell downstairs
4 He fell off the bed
5 A swing hit him in the tummy.

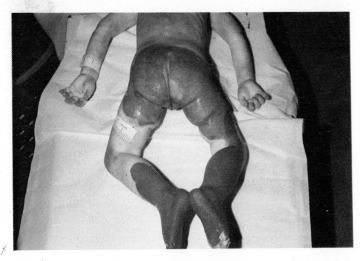

Fig. 2.1. Classical scald burns as a result of immersion in boiling water. Note the absence of burning on reflection of the legs but nevertheless the extensive bruising associated with the outer aspect of the left knee.

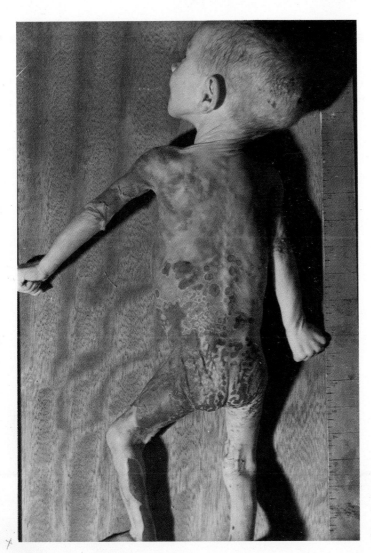

Fig. 2.10. Extensive napkin erythema with pock-like scars from old healed ulceration extending over the genitalia, perineum and the soles of the feet.

On some occasions the injuries will speak for
themselves, either by their nature or pattern. In others,
the mechanism of a fracture may be capable of
interpretation. Injury to the mucosa of the upper lip
(Fig. 2.3) seen in some cases is almost diagnostic.

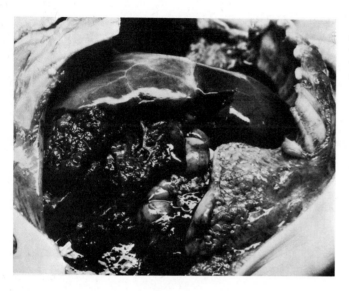

Fig. 2.2. Extensive rupture
of the liver and bruising of
the mesentery as a result of
violence having been applied
to the upper abdomen.

Fig. 2.3 (Left). Classical injury to the mucosa of the upper
lip as a result of an upward blow to the face.
Fig. 2.4 (Right). The back of a child showing the classical areas
of bruising of varying age over the body together with a moderate
nappy rash.

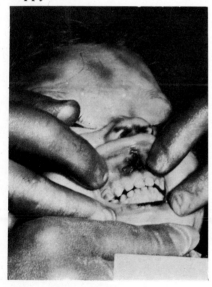
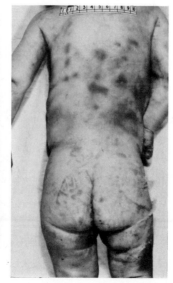

Although bruises are a prominent feature and give rise to the statement 'he bruises easily', care must be given in interpreting their cause (Figs. 2.4 and 2.5). Gripping a child will cause four or five bruises and these, as well as photographs of them, can give a false impression. The serious ones are those that matter and their age. Clearly the basis of approach to each case must be first to save the life of the child by treating the immediate injury, while at the same time being aware of the possibility of aggravation of an older lesion such as secondary bleeding from a subdural haemorrhage. Upon completion of a post-mortem examination, and ideally after a period of 12 to 24 hours refrigeration, it is of value to re-examine the exterior of the child's body, for, frequently, with the progressive blanching of the skin, better delineation of surface bruises beneath the skin surface is revealed and even pattern injuries not noted on earlier examination.

The clinical pathology typical of the battered child can be summarized as follows:

Surface Marks. These consist of bruises, abrasions and burns, of different colours and clearly of different ages, indicative of repeated incidents. They may, however, give an exaggerated idea of the degree of violence due to the fact that children do bruise easily. The important factor, however, is their distribution. Bruises of the scalp are not always clearly visible but may be discovered by palpation and by reaction to tenderness.

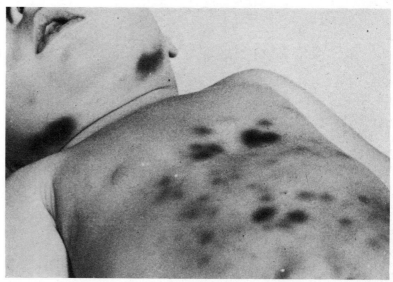

Fig. 2.5. Shows an area of bruising of varying age (similar to that shown in Fig. 2.4) over the front of the upper chest and lower face.

At autopsy, however, on reflection of the scalp, deep
bruising is often detected (Fig. 2.6). In cases of
extensive third degree thermal burns due to immersion
in a bath of hot tap water, the extension of the burns
on to the soles of the feet is enough basis for initially
doubting the allegation of an upturned pan of water.
The presence in almost 50 per cent of cases of
lacerations of the mucosa of the inner aspect of the
upper lip near the frenulum, sometimes with tearing of
the lip from the alveolar margin of the gum (Fig. 2.7),
is now considered almost pathognomic (Cameron *et al*,
1966). This injury is thought to be the result of a blow
on the mouth or of other efforts to silence a screaming
or crying child.

The limbs frequently show 'finger-tip' bruises,
commonly grouped around the elbows and knees, due to
gripping of the child, so as to shake or pull him or to
hurl him into his cot or against furniture, while more
diffuse bruises may be due to blows or impacts by, or
against a surface. Bruising of the chest and trunk may
be due to blows, while bruising of the abdominal wall is
often minimal in spite of severe intra-abdominal injury.
It is often difficult, due to shock and peripheral vascular
failure, to age the bruises with accuracy. Recent cases
(Fig. 2.8a, 2.8b and 2.8c) show an increasing incidence
of bite-marks (Sims, Grant and Cameron, 1973).

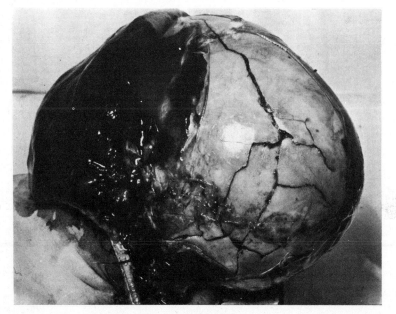

Fig. 2.6. Extensive deep
bruising over the scalp on
reflection with an underlying
extensive fracture of the skull.

Note the absence of any specific changes of avitaminosis, such as a rickety rosary, even with cases exhibiting a wizzened appearance of the trunk and extremities associated with marked atrophy of the extremities and concavity of the cheeks and chronic depletion of the subcutaneous fat. Frequently the abdomen is markedly sunken with the ribs presenting an unusually prominent front-to-back diameter; the back and buttocks and lower extremities show a severe

Fig. 2.7. A severe example of the tearing of the upper lip extending along the alveolar margin which occurred three days prior to death. There is also evidence of an older injury to the mouth in the form of a tooth having been knocked out and scarring of the gum as a result approximately 3–4 months earlier.

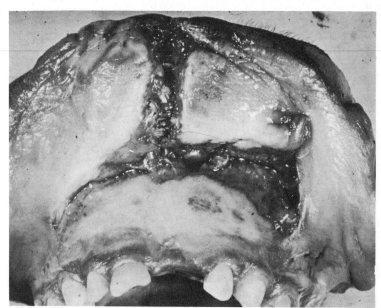

Fig. 2.8a. Marks consistent with adult human dentition the buttocks of a young boy.

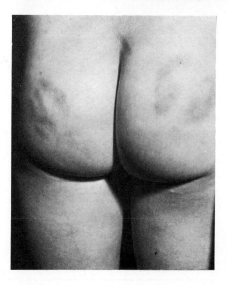

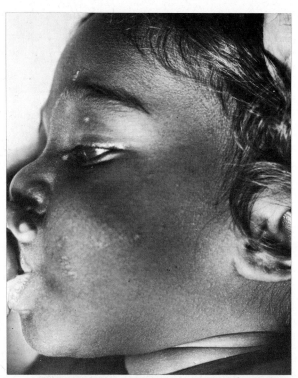

Fig. 2.8b. A photograph taken under ultra-violet light showing evidence of marks consistent with having been caused by adult dentition over the prominence of the left cheek.

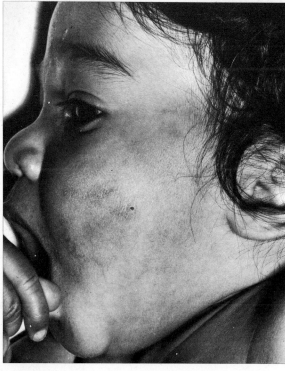

weeping infected napkin erythema (Fig. 2.9), which, in some cases, even extends over the soles of the feet which are secondarily infected with 'pock-like' scars of healed ulceration, often associated with weeping denudation of the skin of the genitalia and perineum (Fig. 2.10).
Skeletal Injuries. In view of the usual intermittent nature of the trauma radiological examination of fractures may reveal various stages of reparative change. On the other hand, if no fractures or dislocations are apparent on examination, it must always be remembered that bone injury may be difficult to detect during the

Fig. 2.9. Extensive napkin erythema of the weeping variety associated with a degree of scalding.

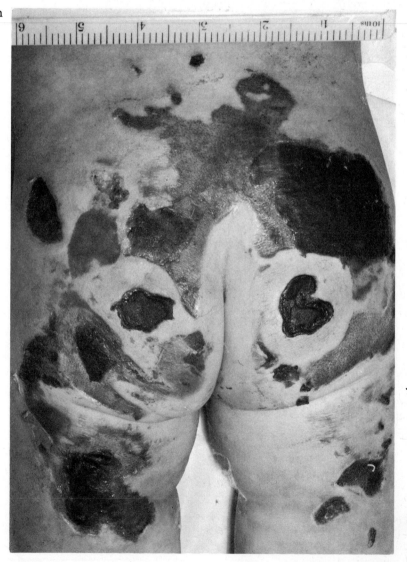

first few days after inflicted trauma. In life, as documented in the historic observations of the classical descriptions of the battered baby, the radiologist may be the first to call attention to the existence of pre-existing trauma in a child suffering from acute violence. It should be carefully understood, however, by all working in the field that the assistance of the radiologist is invaluable: not only may he date and serialise bone injuries on the trunk more accurately than the pathologist but in those portions of the body which the pathologist is often reluctant, for aesthetic reasons, to examine, he may document injuries hitherto unsuspected.

The forces applied in grasping and seizing the child will usually involve traction and torsion; such strains and stresses will produce epiphyseal separations and periosteal shearing, while fractures of the shafts of the long bones may result from direct trauma, bending, compressing or twisting (see Chapter 3).

Visceral Injuries. Analysis of the fatal injuries show that predominantly they are associated with the head and, as an alternative, with a ruptured liver. If proper objective consideration is given to this pattern, the terminal injuries are nearly always seen to be a subdural haemorrhage with or without a fractured skull, and, at the same time, in many cases, compression of the chest with fractured ribs and ruptured viscera. The commonest cause of infantile subdural haemorrhage (Guthkelch, 1971) is rupture of one or more of the delicate bridging veins which run from the cerebral cortex to the venous sinuses, the mode of injury being either a single acceleration or deceleration due to a heavy moving object striking the head or the rapidly moving head being brought up against a stationary mass; multiple applications of force would increase the total strain on the bridging veins and might result in an increased incidence of rupture. Subdural haematoma is one of the commonest features of the battered child syndrome, yet by no means all the patients so affected have external marks of injury on the head. This suggests that in some cases repeated acceleration/decelaration rather than direct violence is the cause of the haemorrhage, the infant having been shaken rather than struck by its parent. Such a hypothesis might also explain the remarkable frequency of the finding of subdural haemorrhage in battered children as compared with its incidence in head injuries of other origin, and the fact that it is so often bilateral. Rupture of the liver and abdominal viscera with tearing of the mesentery is seen but external bruising of the abdominal wall is not necessarily present—a reminder that a diffuse blow to the relaxed abdomen may cause severe internal injury and yet leave no external mark.

An explanation for the high incidence of visceral injuries, near a relatively fixed point in the mid-abdomen, is offered by Haller (1966) who distinguishes the causes of blunt abdominal trauma by the mechanism of injury. He notes that crushing or compressing forces produce bursting injuries of the liver or spleen or they may cause perforation of a distended hollow viscus, such as the stomach, intestine or bladder. Intestinal injuries are usually on the anti-mesenteric surface. A decelerating force, such as a punch or blow, tears the mesentery and may disrupt the small intestine at sites of ligamental support. The galaxy of visceral injuries in battered children best fits the latter category (Touloukian, 1968).

The possibility of visceral injury from blunt trauma should be eliminated in any child with abdominal complaints who has characteristic bruising whether or not skeletal fractures or a head injury are present. A specific history of abdominal trauma may be remote or non-existent. Even if it is elicited, there may be a variable period of well-being preceding the onset of abdominal complaints.

Ocular Injuries. Permanent impairment of vision affecting one or both eyes is now a well recognized complication of battered children (Kiffney, 1964; Gilkes and Mann, 1967; Maroteaux, Fessard and Aron, 1967; Maroteaux and Lamy, 1967; Mushin and Morgan, 1970; Mushin, 1971). Ocular disease, especially retinal haemorrhage, is common in this syndrome, and infants considered to have been battered should always have a complete opthalmic examination. Trauma should be especially considered in pseudoglioma, Coat's disease, lens dislocation and all forms of old or recent intra-ocular haemorrhages (see Chapter 4).

SOCIAL ASPECTS

Ill-treatment of children by parental abuse or neglect may occur at any age, but when the child is under three years of age it cannot relate how the trauma was inflicted and older children in the family are reluctant or afraid to tell the story. Hence the age is of significance, especially when the history given by the parents is at variance with the clinical picture and the physical signs noted on objective examination of the child; together with these is the knowledge that no new lesions occur during the child's hospitalisation. Closer questioning frequently reveals that the child has been taken to various hospitals and doctors in an attempt to negate any suspicion of parental abuse. Often they give a complete denial of any knowledge of inflicted trauma. This difficulty in obtaining any type of history leaves the diagnosis dependant upon physical examination, radiological findings and a low threshold of suspicion on the part of the clinician, pathologist or police.

Often the victim is an unwanted child, for example, the result of pregnancy before marriage, or where there is doubt of the father's paternity, or where the child is 'in the way', or where there is infidelity or suspicion of it.

There is frequently a history of family discord, long-standing emotional problems, or financial stress, although the character and personality of the guilty parent, commonly aged between 20 and 30, need not give outward signs of neurosis or psychosis; on the contrary, he or she may present the rather disarming attitude of co-operativeness, over-protectiveness and neatness. Many of the fathers have criminal records and are unemployed at the time of the incident (Skinner and Castle, 1969) and the mother is frequently pregnant or in the premenstrual period at the time of battering. Court (1970) reports that many support the view that the 'innocent' partner in a battering situation is always consciously or unconsciously aware of what is happening. In many cases the partner must have been present when the actual episode took place.

Parents who mistreat their children in the manner characteristic of battering are rarely schizophrenic or psychopathic. They are generally young and are found at all levels of social class, intelligence and education. Characteristically their standards of appearance, speech and social manner are high. The underlying personality defect appears to be a temporary or permanent deficiency of the feelings of affection, acceptance and approval which normal parents have toward children, combined with a positive tendency to give violent expression to tension.

Battering can, and occasionally does, occur in well-to-do families who do not have any adverse social problems. However, most of those involved come from the lower income groups where social deprivation adds greatly to the danger of child battering in families in which the parents are psychologically at risk. Financial hardship and intolerable housing conditions add to the strains and tensions in any marriage, and place impossible demands on the vulnerable parents' already limited reserves. The difficulties of tolerating a crying baby at night and consequent loss of sleep may increase the possibility of aggressive outbursts to such an extent as to produce the 'crying child syndrome'.

The syndrome is not confined to children of parents with a psychopathic personality or a border-line socio-economic status but, in most cases, there is some defect in character structure. According to Fairburn and Hunt (1964) the rejection of the child is probably a constant feature starting for the mother either with the first realisation of pregnancy or during an anxious or painful puerperium or when the infant is fractious for long periods; or for the father if, for some reason, he doubts the child's paternity. Guilt amnesia is a well-recognised condition in most of the abusive parents (Cameron et al, 1966; Cameron, 1970, 1972).

Dawson (1970) put a further view when she pointed out that the state of motherhood has undergone a change in the last two decades. On the one hand, the mother's and her baby's health have received more attention through the National Health Service; but, on the other, a mother has never before been left so alone. Modern life has placed intolerable burdens on the mother of a young family—burdens she frequently has to carry alone. There appears to be certain periods when the risk is greater, such as during pregnancy or in the premenstrual phase of her cycle. The child is also at risk during early infancy particularly if persistently crying, wet or dirty. His very inability to co-operate can easily evoke rage rather than understanding and love. Help is what is required.

REFERENCES

Altman, D. H., and Smith, R. L. (1960) *J. Bone and Joint Surg*. **42A**, 407.
Caffey, J. (1946) *Amer. J. Roentgenol* **56**, 163.
Caffey, J. (1957) *Brit. J. Radiol*. **30**, 225.
Cameron, J. M. (1970) *Btit. J. Hosp. Med*. **4**, 769.
Cameron, J. M. (1972) *Practitioner* **209**, 302.
Cameron, J. M. (1974) *Prevent* 1972/3 **1** No. 5/6 p.59.
Cameron, J. M., Johnson, H. R. M. and Camps, F. E. (1966) *Med. Sci. and L*. **6**, 2.
Cooper, C. E. (1970) *J. Med. Wom. Fed*., **52**, 93.
Court, J. (1970) *J. Med. Wom. Fed*., **53**, 93.
Dawson, D. (1970) *The Scotsman*. January 19th.
Fairburn, A. C. and Hunt, A. C. (1964) *Med. Sci. and L*. **4**, 123.
Fleming, G. M. (1967) *Brit. Med. J*. **2**, 421.
Fontana, V. J., Donavan, D. and Wong, R. J. (1963) *New Engl. J. Med* **269**, 1389.
Gilkes, M. J. and Mann, T. P. (1967) *Lancet* **2**, 468.
Griffiths, D. L. and Moynihan, F. J. (1963) *Brit. Med. J*. **2**, 1558.
Guthkelch, A. N. (1971) *Brit. Med. J*. **1**, 430.
Gwinn, J. L., Lewin, K. W. and Paterson, H. G, Jr. (1961) *J. Amer. Med. Assoc*. **176**, 926.
Haller, J. A. Jr. (1966) *Clin. Pediat*. (Phila.) **5**, 476.
Kempe, C. H. (1970) Unpublished.
Kempe, C. H., Silverman, F. N., Steele, B. F., Droegenuelleur, W, M. and Silver, H. K. (1962) *J. Amer Med. Ass*. **181**, 17.
Kiffney, G. T. Jr., (1964) Arch. of *Opthal*. **72**, 231.
Maroteaux, P., Fessard, C., and Aron, J. J. (1967) *Presse Medicale*, **75**, 711.
Maroteaux, P. and Lawry, M. (1967) *Lancet* **2**, 829.
Mushin, A. S. and Morgan, G. (1970) *Brit. J. Ophthal*. **55**, 343.
Mushin, A. S. (1971) *Brit. Med. J*. **3**, 402.
Silverman, F. N. (1953) *Amer. J. Roentgenol*. **69**, 413.
Simpson, C. K. (1965) *The Battered Child Syndrome*. London: NSPCC.
Sims, B. G., Grant, J. H. and Cameron, J. M. (1973) *Med. Sci. and L*. **13**, 207.
Skinner, A. E. and Castle, R. L. (1969) *78 Battered Children: a retrospective study*, London: NSPCC.
Touloukian, R. J. (1968) *Pediatrics*. **42**, 642.
Woolley, P. V. J. and Evans W. A. Jr. (1955) *J. Amer. Med. Ass*. **158**, 539.

3. The Radiological Diagnosis

One diagnostic radiological feature of the battered baby syndrome is the avulsion injury of the metaphysis caused by jerking the baby up by a limb or swinging the baby while grasping the wrist or ankle. Another diagnostic feature is the presence of multiple rib fractures caused by compression of the chest or by direct violence. Neither of these injuries can be caused by a simple or accidental fall from a cot or pram or by being dropped, the explanations commonly given by the parent or by the person responsible for the care of the baby.

The presence of multiple fractures of the long bones in varying stages of healing, indicating more than one traumatic incident, is suggestive of abuse, but is not definite proof of the battered baby syndrome.

One must exclude bone disease, such as osteogensis imperfecta, or spina bifida where the bones are porotic, and where fractures resulting from slight accidental trauma can resemble those caused by non-accidental injury.

Although in these cases there may be a strong suspicion clinically of a battered baby syndrome, one cannot say from the radiological examination that the fractures are not due to accidental trauma.

RADIOGRAPHIC EXAMINATION

Any unusual skeletal injury or an injury, the severity of which is not compatible with the history, warrants a complete skeletal survey. This is performed to establish the full extent of the injuries with special reference to the metaphyses and ribs, and to ascertain whether there are any old injuries, indicating previous traumatic incidents. This survey does not entail unwarranted excessive radiation. As the majority of battered babies are under the age of one year a complete survey can be obtained with three exposures. One exposure is made of lateral view of the skull, another of the upper half of the body to include the arms down to the wrists and fingers and the third of the rest of the body, including the ankles and feet. The exposure of the upper half of the body must be such as to produce a film of sufficient penetration to show the posterior aspects of the ribs through the mediastinal shadow. If on the films there is any suggestion of an injury, however small, then a further radiograph of this area should be taken. This applies especially to the necks of the ribs where recent or healed fractures will be more clearly demonstrated by taking views from different angles. This statement may appear obvious but it is made intentionally to emphasise the necessity, in a case of a suspected battered baby of establishing a definite diagnosis which may have important consequences on the baby's future.

HEAD INJURIES

If a baby falls, the commonest skeletal injury is a fracture of the skull, usually of the parieto-occipital region. A fracture sustained in this way does not differ from that resulting from a non-accidental injury, so that in a case where a fracture of the skull is the only skeletal injury (Fig. 3.1) or where there is evidence of a subdural haematoma, as shown by suture diastasis, with or without a fracture (Fig. 3.2), one cannot say whether this results from accidental or from

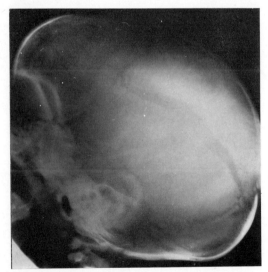

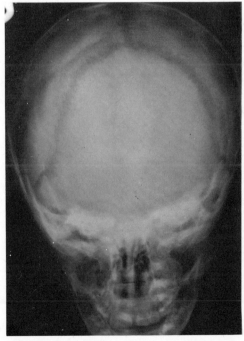

Fig. 3.1. Extensive fracture of the parietal bone. This could have resulted from an accidental or a non-accidental injury. This is a common site for a fracture resulting from a simple fall, but it could equally have been caused by an assualt.

Fig. 3.2. Diastasis of the sutures due to a subdural haematoma. There is no fracture.

non-accidental trauma. If, however, the fracture of the
skull is associated with a metaphysial injury or with
multiple rib fractures, then the evidence is that of a
battered baby. On the contrary, in a case of a fracture
of the skull associated with a fracture of the diaphysis
of a long bone, although this may suggest a battered
baby syndrome, such a firm diagnosis of the syndrome
cannot be made on the radiological evidence.
There are several suture variants in the skull which
must be distinguished from fractures. These variants are
usually bilateral, but may be unilateral when one side
has fused; in such a case there may be some difficulty
in making a diagnosis (Figs. 3.3 to 3.6).

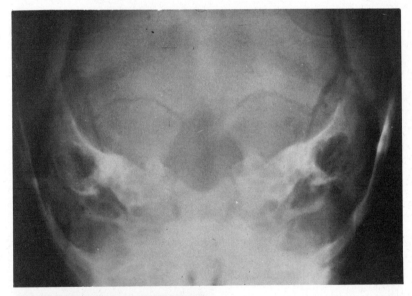

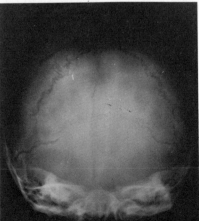

Fig. 3.3 (above). Suture
variant; synchondrosis
between the ex-occipital and
supra-occipital bones.

Fig. 3.4 (left). Suture
variant; Mendosal suture,
running across the occipital
bone.

A

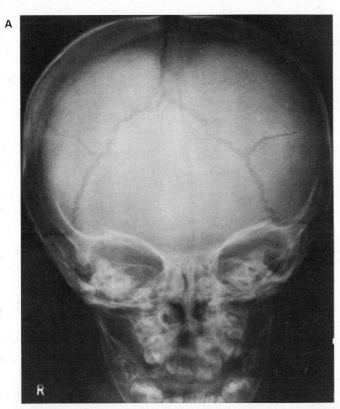

B

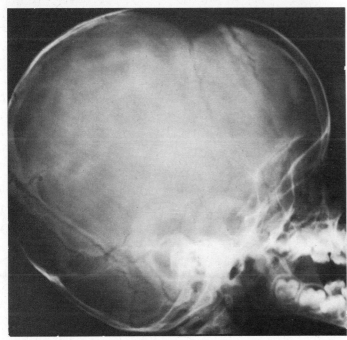

Fig. 3.5. Suture variant; bifid-parietal or intra-parietal suture, running forwards into the parietal bone from the lambdoid suture. There is a fracture in the left suture with diastasis of the sagittal suture.
(a) Anterio-posterior view
(b) Lateral view

Fig. 3.6. An unusual suture
variant, running alongside of
the lambdoid suture.
(a) Right side: oblique view
(b) Left side: oblique view

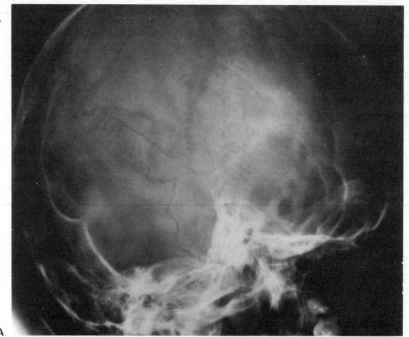

A

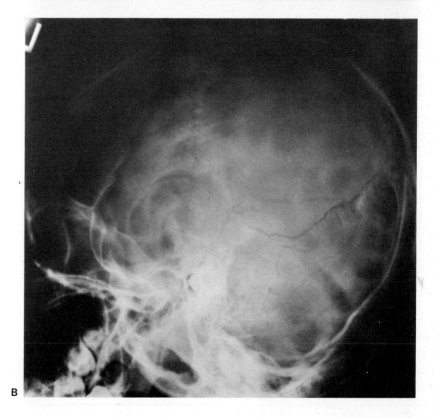

B

METAPHYSIAL INJURIES

These occur in the region of the joints of the limbs and are caused by the baby being held by the arms or legs and jerked violently upwards or forwards, or by the baby being swung by the arms or legs and then thrown down. This sudden jerk, or wrench, of the limb causes an avulsion injury of the metaphysis and epiphysis. The periosteum is torn from its firm attachment to the epiphysial cartilage; haemorrhage occurs and strips the periosteum off from its loose attachment to the diaphysis, forming a subperiosteal haematoma. The metaphysis may be fractured (Figs. 3.7 and 3.8); small pieces of bone may be detached from the metaphysis (Figs. 3.9 and 3.10) or the metaphysial surface may be rendered uneven or fragmented (Figs. 3.11, 3.12 and 3.13). The normal appearance of beaking should not be mistaken for that due to injury (Fig. 3.14). These lesions tend to be more common in the lower limbs, the probable reason being that it is easier and quicker to grasp a leg rather than an arm when the baby is lying on its back.

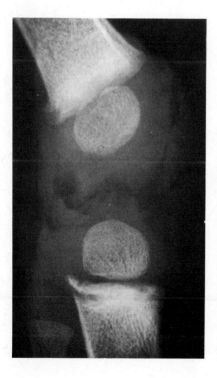
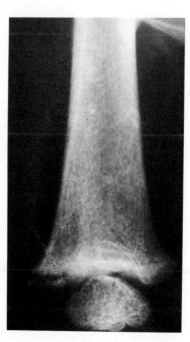

Fig. 3.7 (left). Avulsion fractures of the distal metaphysis of the femur and of the proximal metaphysis of the tibia. When the fracture is intra-articular no external callus is demonstrable, so that the age of the injury cannot be accurately estimated.

Fig. 3.8 (right). Avulsion fracture of the distal metaphysis of the femur, mainly intra-articular. There was also a fracture of the shaft of this femur and several other metaphysial injuries.

Fig. 3.9 (left). Small fragment of bone, detached from the posterior aspect of the distal metaphysis of the femur. This is the so-called 'cut off corner' appearance which is not uncommon in an avulsion injury.

Fig. 3.10 (right). Fragment of bone detached from the medial aspect of the distal metaphysis of the femur. There were other metaphysial injuries and a healed fractured rib in this baby.

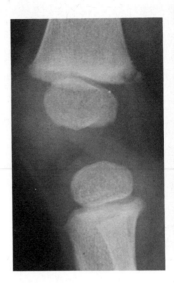
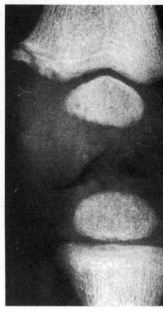

Fig. 3.11 (left). Irregularity of the border of the proximal metaphysis of the left tibia caused by swinging the baby by the legs. There was also a subdural haematoma present.

Fig. 3.12 (right). Irregularity of the border of the distal metaphysis of the femur with detached fragments of bone. There were several other bone injuries of varying ages and a marked diastasis of the skull sutures. This is a macrogram, a method which can be applied with advantage.

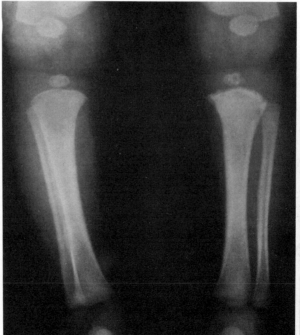
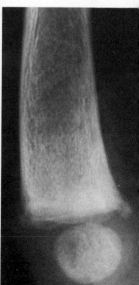

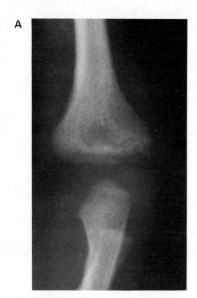

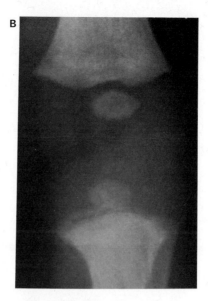

Fig. 3.13 (above).
(a) Irregularity of the distal
metaphysis of the humerus.
(b) Irregularity of the
proximal metaphysis of the
tibia in the same patient.

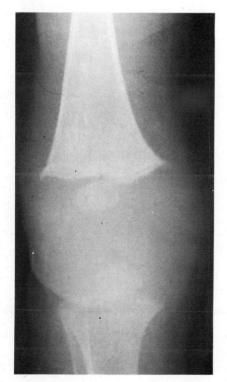

Fig. 3.14. Normal beaking of
the distal metaphysis of the
femur.

Where the periosteum has been lifted from the underlying bone by haematoma, periosteal new bone formation will take place; this can be demonstrated radiologically seven to ten days following the trauma (Figs. 3.15 to 3.20). The extent of this new bone formation depends on the severity of the trauma and the degree of haemorrhage. It may extend along the whole length of the shaft, especially where both the proximal and distal metaphyses have been damaged (Fig. 3.21).

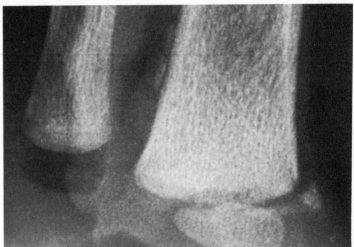

Fig. 3.15. Fragment of bone detached from the distal metaphysis of the tibia with early periosteal new bone formation extending along the diaphysis. The estimated age of the injury is 7 to 10 days.

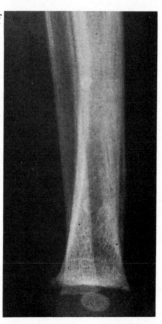
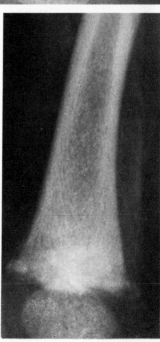

Fig. 3.16 (left). Fragments of bone detached from the distal metaphysis of the tibia with periosteal new bone formation along the shaft.

Fig. 3.17 (right). Early calcification in a subperiosteal haematoma with metaphysial damage at the distal end of the femur. The estimated age of this injury is 7 to 10 days. A similar appearance can be present in a case of scurvy (see Fig. 4.10).

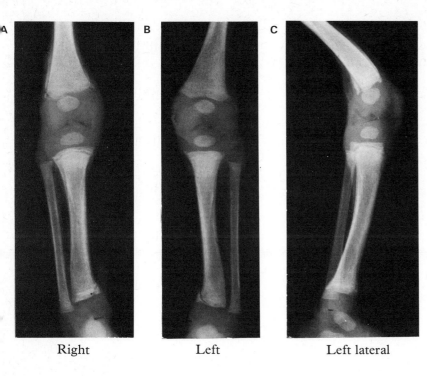

Right   Left   Left lateral

Fig. 3.18. The lower limbs of a female infant age 4 months.
(a) Small pieces of bone detached from the distal femoral and the proximal tibial metaphyses with no new bone visible. Larger fragment detached from the distal tibial metaphysis with early new bone formation. The estimated age of this injury is 7 to 10 days. It can be assumed that the injuries around the knee joint occurred at the same time.
(b) Injuries to the distal femoral and the proximal tibial metaphyses of the left knee with new bone formation, which is more advanced than that in the right leg, making the age of the injury rather older than the 10 days.
(c) Lateral view of the left knee, showing that the damage is slightly more extensive than seen in the antero-posterior view.

Fig. 3.19. The knees of a female infant aged 3 months, showing metaphysial injuries and calcification in a subperiosteal haematoma on the posterior aspect of the distal end of the left femur. The estimated age of the injury is 2 weeks. This baby was swung by the legs and thrown, sustaining, in addition to the metaphysial injuries, multiple rib fractures and a subdural haematoma from which she died.
(a) Right knee.
(b) Left knee.
(c) Lateral view of left knee.

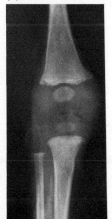

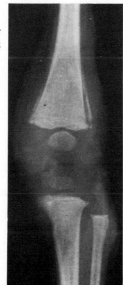

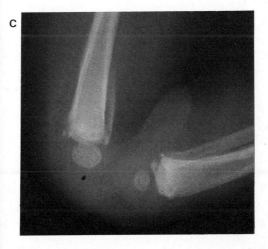

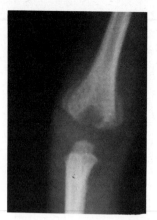 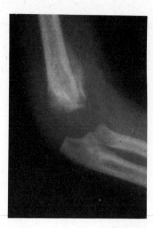

Fig. 3.20 (above).
Metaphysial injury of distal
end of the humerus with
calcification in a subperiosteal
haematoma. This injury is
about 3 weeks old.

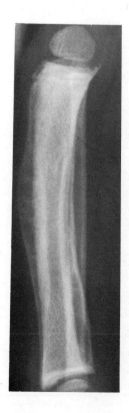

Fig. 3.21 (right). Periosteal
new bone extending along the
whole length of the shaft of
the tibia with proximal and
distal metaphysial injuries.
This appearance bears some
resemblance to Caffey's
disease (see Fig. 4.16), except
for the metaphysial injuries.

Usually in the case of a metaphysial injury the new bone extends to the epiphysial plate but may continue round the end of the metaphysis between this and the epiphysis giving rise to the so-called 'bucket handle' appearance (Figs. 3.22, 3.23 and 3.24). Cases can occur where the new bone stops short of the metaphysis (Figs. 3.25 and 3.26). This may be due to a firmer attachment of the periosteum or it could occur in cases where the trauma is directed more to the diaphysis, such as grasping the infant by the middle of the leg rather than by the foot. In these cases the appearances may resemble those of infantile cortical hyperostosis of Caffey*, especially where there are no metaphysial changes (see Fig. 4.19). In cases where the trauma is severe the haemorrhage and subsequent bone formation may invade the surrounding soft tissues (Figs. 27 and 28), giving rise to appearances which can resemble those of scurvy (see Fig. 4.12).

Fig. 3.22 (left). The 'bucket-handle' appearance where the new bone extends round the end of the metaphysis between this and the epiphysial plate, at the distal end of the tibia.

Fig. 3.23 (right). The 'bucket-handle' appearance at the proximal end of the tibia. This could be a fracture of the metaphysis.

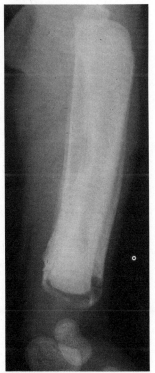 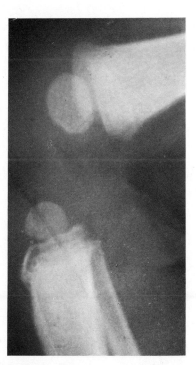

*Hereafter referred to in the text as Caffey's disease.

Fig. 24. Injuries of the distal metaphyses of both tibiae with early 'bucket-handle' appearance in a battered 8 month old female infant. There is also periosteal new bone extending along the shafts, resembling the appearances seen in Caffey's disease (see Fig. 4.16) and in congenital syphilis (see Fig. 4.12) except for the metaphysial injuries. The mother confessed to gripping the baby by the ankles and violently jerking her upwards out of the cot. There were several other skeletal injuries present.

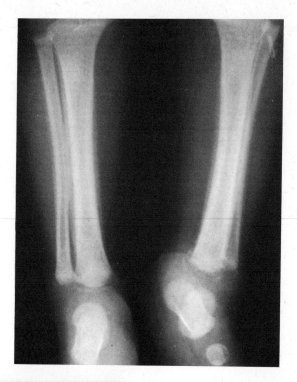

Fig. 3.25 (left). Periosteal new bone on the shaft of the tibia not extending to the metaphysis in a case of a battered baby. Even when there is a metaphysial injury the periosteal new bone does not always extend to the metaphysis; this is due to a firmer attachment of the periosteum in the region of the metaphysis.

Fig. 3.26 (right). Fragments of bone detached from the distal metaphysis of the tibia with a linear fracture of the diaphysis. The periosteal new bone along the shaft could result from either or both of these injuries. There is also a dislocation of the tibio-fibular joint.

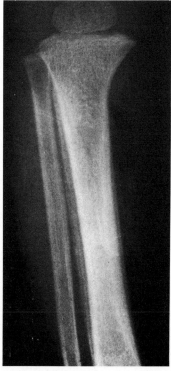

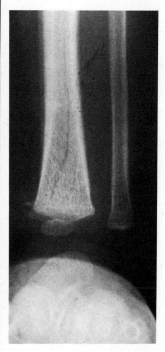

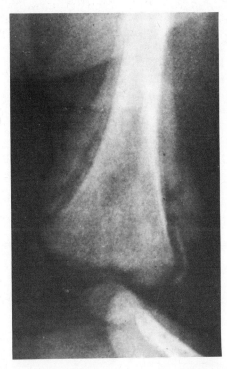

Fig. 3.27. Metaphysial injury of the distal end of the femur with extensive calcification in the surrounding soft tissues in a male infant aged 4 months. These appearances resemble those occurring in a case of scurvy (see Fig. 4.9), but it should be remembered that scurvy is uncommon under the age of 5 months. A similar appearance can occur following an avulsion injury caused during labour where the leg presents.

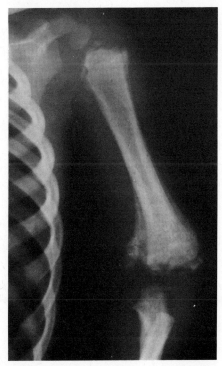

Fig. 3.28. Injury of the distal metaphysis of the humerus with calcification in the soft tissues resulting from avulsion. There is also an injury of the proximal metaphysis.

Estimation of the age of the injury

This becomes important should any doubt arise as to the veracity of the parents' statements regarding the date of the injury. It is also of importance to establish whether there has been more than one traumatic incident. As soon as the new bone becomes visible radiologically one can, as a general rule, estimate the age of the injury at seven to ten days. There are exceptions, as where the fracture is intra-articular and the formation of the new bone may not be evident (see Fig. 3.8); also the formation of the new bone may be delayed as in cases of malnutrition. Following its first appearance from seven to ten days after the trauma, the periosteal new bone forms rapidly and in one to four months the appearance can be that of thickened cortex (Fig. 3.29).

Fig. 3.29. Consolidating periosteal new bone 4 weeks after an injury.

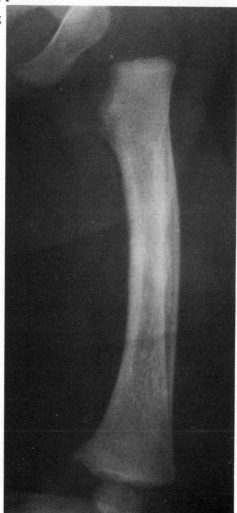

There is, however, no standard appearance of the progress and consolidation of the new bone so that one can only give a rough estimate of the age of the injury according to one's experience (Fig. 3.30). Periosteal new bone occurs normally and can be seen in over 40 per cent of premature and full term babies, most commonly on the shafts of the femur, humerus and tibia. It is always bilateral, though it may be more prominent on one side. It is mostly confined to the diaphysis but may extend to the metaphysis though never beyond. The underlying bone is normal (Figs. 3.31 and 3.32). Caffey has suggested (1946) that it might be the result of slight trauma, for example, during the routine handling of the baby, but there is no real proof of this. The appearances should be considered as essentially normal. In a case of injury, a distinction must be made between this normal bone layer and the pathological new bone resulting from the trauma. In the case of trauma, the normal layer may be interrupted by a fracture or by haemorrhage (Fig. 3.33). When the pathological new bone forms later it will be as a continuous, unbroken layer superimposed upon the normal one (Fig. 3.34). This distinction is of importance when estimating the age of injury. In Figure

Fig. 3.30. Metaphysial injury of the distal end of the femur with a small piece of bone detached. These radiographs illustrate the extent of the new bone which subsequently forms and acts as a guide to the estimation of the age of the injury. The radiographs were taken at the following intervals after the injury:
(a) 1 day.   (b) 2 weeks.   (c) 3 weeks.   (d) 5 weeks.

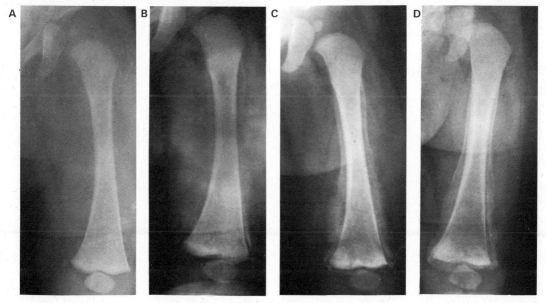

Fig. 3.31. Normal formation of periosteal new bone on the shafts of the femora.

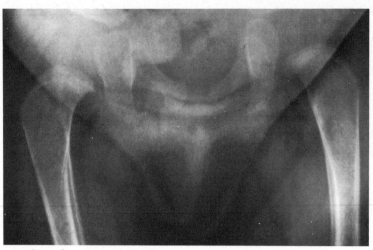

Fig. 3.32 (left). Normal formation of periosteal new bone on the medial and lateral aspects of the shafter of the femur.

Fig. 3.33 (middle). Fracture of the femur breaking the continuity of the normal periosteal new bone layer; there is no pathological new bone visible indicating that the injury is less than a week old; in fact the injury was 1 day old.

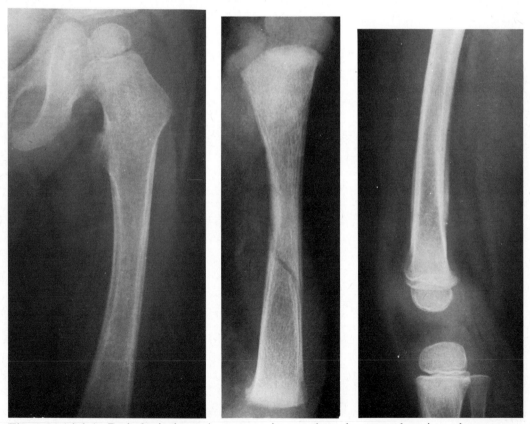

Fig. 3.34 (right). Pathological new bone superimposed on the normal periosteal new bone layer and showing as a distinct separate layer.

3.33 there is no pathological new bone visible, so that one can say that the injury is less than one week old. Deformities resulting from metaphysial injuries may persist for some time and it is important that they should be recognised. In a case of the battered baby syndrome any deformity, however slight, should not be disregarded (Fig. 3.35). The older the injury the less noticeable will the deformity become (Fig. 3.36). Any of the above mentioned metaphysial injuries may be so small as to be considered of no importance, but it cannot be emphasised too strongly that any injury in the region of a metaphysis, be it a small crack or a small piece of detached bone, in a case of a suspected battered baby, should in the first instance be regarded as having resulted from a non-accidental injury.

A

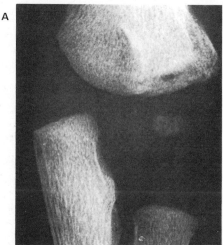

Fig. 3.35. Slight deformities resulting from metaphysial injuries of the distal end of the humerus (A) and of the distal end of the tibia (B) in the same patient. Both injuries are from 4 to 6 weeks old.

Fig. 3.36 (below). Slight deformity resulting from a metaphysial injury of the lateral aspect of the distal end of the humerus 3 months after the injury.

B

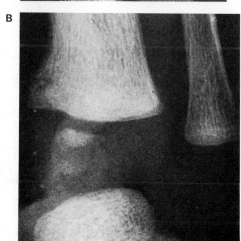

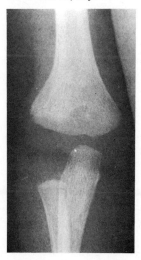

RIB INJURIES

Multiple fractures of ribs are a common feature in the battered baby. It is unusual for a baby to sustain a fracture of a rib by falling from a cot or pram or by being dropped, and very rare to sustain multiple fractures. Multiple fractures can occur in vehicular accidents and in cases where there is a pathological bone lesion such as osteogensis imperfecta (see Fig. 4.4). In the battered baby the common site of these fractures is in the posterior aspect, often close to the spine and frequently bilateral. They are caused by lateral compression, such as violent squeezing of the chest from side to side; this action tends to make the ribs spring and fracture at their fixed points posteriorly (Figs. 3.37 and 3.38). Fractures of the costo-chondral junctions may be associated, though less commonly, and are caused by the same mechanism (Figs. 3.37 and 3.38). Antero-posterior compression is more likely to cause fractures in the mid-axillary line (Figs. 3.39 and 3.40).

Fig. 3.37 (left). Multiple fractures of the ribs in the posterior aspects and of the costochondral junctions. The ages of these fractures vary from 2 to 4 weeks.

Fig. 3.38 (right). Multiple fractures of the ribs in the posterior aspects and of the costochondral junctions. These fractures are mostly about 3 weeks old.

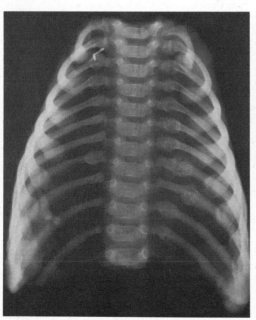 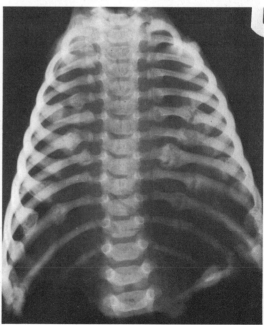

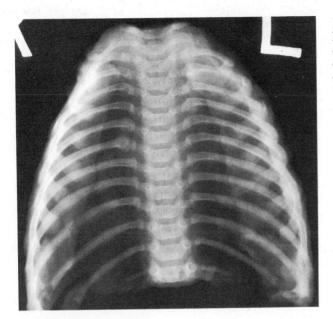

Fig. 3.39. Fractures of the left ribs in the axillary line due to antero-posterior compression. There are also one or two older fractures of the necks.

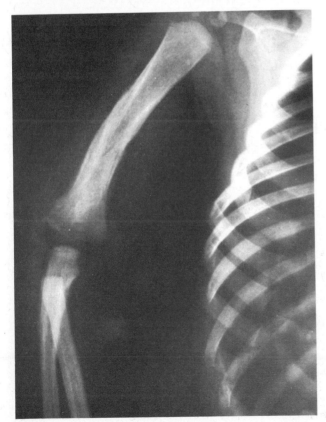

Fig. 3.40. Old fracture of the humerus and recent fractures of the ribs in the axillary line.

This site is the least common in the battered baby syndrome, but a fracture has been known to occur when this compression has been applied in a case of cardiac arrest. Direct violence, as distinct from compression, can also cause fractures of the ribs—violence such as striking the chest with the fist or foot or by swinging the baby by the foot and causing the chest to come into contact by/or against some hard object. The site of a fracture caused in this way will usually be at the point where the violence is applied (Fig. 3.41). Many cases when first radiographed show multiple fractures of the ribs in varying stages of healing, indicating that there has been more than one traumatic incident. The external callus, owing to continuous movement, tends to be excessive and, as healing progresses, a characteristic nodule is formed (Fig. 3.42). When the fracture involves the neck of the rib this bony nodule may not be very distinctive (Fig. 3.43). but an oblique view will show the nodule more clearly as a round area of increased density (Fig. 3.44). This appearance is not present in an oblique view of the neck of a normal rib (Fig. 3.45). When the fracture involves the costo-chondral junction this bony nodule can also be more clearly shown in the oblique and lateral views (Figs. 3.46 and 3.47) when it is not demonstrated in the antero-posterior view (Fig. 3.48). The lateral view is of value in demonstrating this nodule of callus when the appearance of the fracture in the antero-posterior view resembles the changes due to rickets (Fig. 3.49).

Fig. 3.41. Fracture of the anterior aspect of the left first rib with callus formation. This fracture resulted from a direct blow on the front of the chest. Both acromioclavicular joints are dislocated with new bone formation on the outer ends of both clavicles. It is possible that the dislocations resulted from the same injury as that which caused the fracture of the rib.

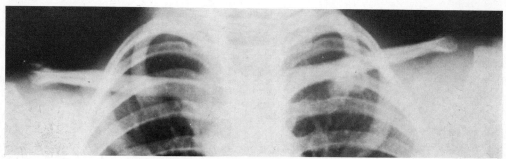

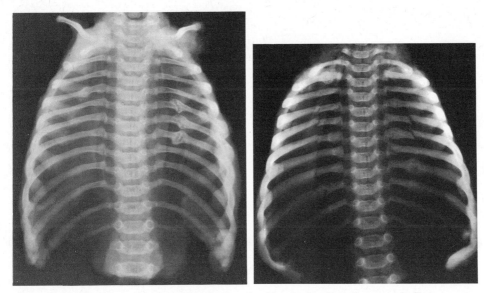

Fig. 3.42 (left). Characteristic nodules of callus in healing fractured ribs.
Fig. 3.43 (right). Antero-posterior view of nodular thickenings in the necks of ribs due to callus formation.

Fig. 3.44 (left). The nodular thickenings of the necks of the right ribs 5 to 9 in the same patient, as in Figure 3.43, shown more prominently in an oblique view.
Fig. 3.45 (centre). This shows the appearance of the necks of normal ribs in an oblique view.
Fig. 3.46 (right). The bony nodules at the site of fractures of the costochondral junctions can be shown more clearly in oblique views than in the antero-posterior.

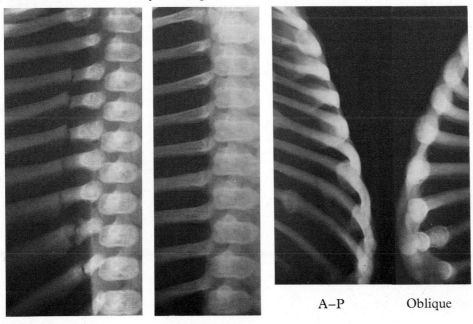

A–P   Oblique

Fig. 3.47. The bony nodules at the site of fractures of the costochondral junctions are shown more clearly in a lateral view when they were not distinctive in the anteroposterior (Fig. 3.48).

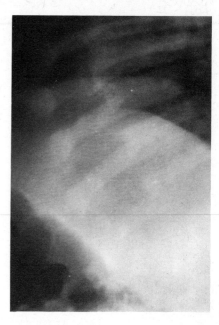

Fig. 3.48 (left). Antero-posterior view of the same patient as in Figure 3.47 showing healing fractures of the costochondral junctions, appearances that could be mistaken for rickets (Fig. 3.49). The lateral view shows the nodular thickening of callus which is not a feature of rickets.

Fig. 3.49 (right). An antero-posterior view of the costochondral junctions in rickets.

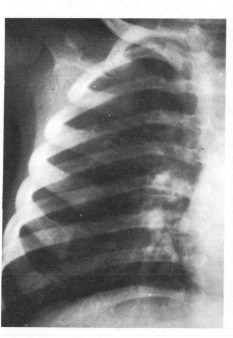
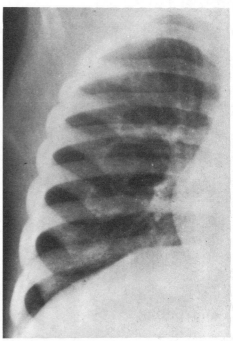

As further healing takes place the nodules become more contracted and less dense and may be almost indistinguishable from the normal (Fig. 3.50). In Figure 3.51 a case is shown where the appearance of the fractured ribs has returned to normal six months after the injury. In some cases recent fractures are not demonstrated unless views are taken from varying angles (Fig. 3.52) and it has been shown that a recent fracture seen as an area of haemorrhage at a

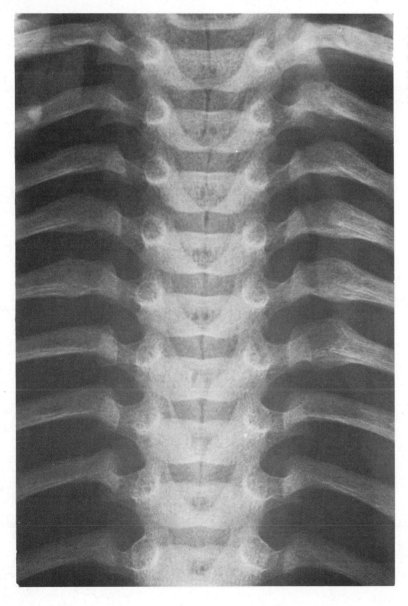

Fig. 3.50. Further healing of the fractures of the necks of the ribs with the bony nodules becoming less distinct. The age of these fractures is 4 weeks or more.

A 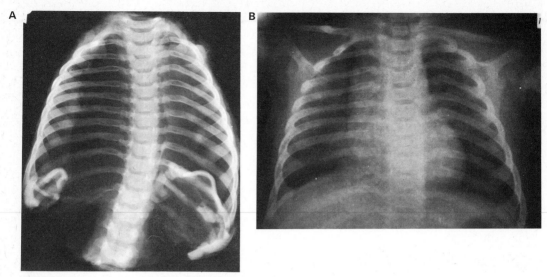 B

Fig. 3.51. (a) Healed fractures of necks of ribs not distinguishable from the normal. (b) The same patient showing the fractures of the necks of the ribs, right 3 and 4 and left 3 and 4 at about 2 to 3 weeks after the injury.

Fig. 3.52. Fractures of the ribs in the anterior axillary line shown in an oblique view when they were ill-defined in the antero-posterior view. Note that the costochondral junctions can appear dense in an oblique view, but this appearance should not be mistaken for nodular thickenings of callus (see Fig. 3.46).

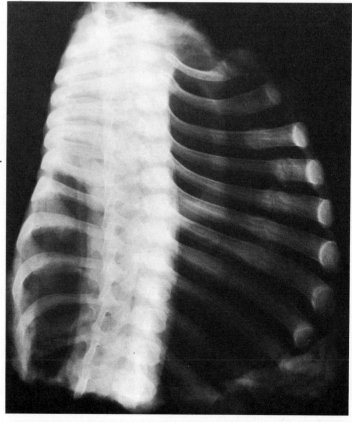

post-mortem examination is not always discernible on
the radiograph of the post-mortem specimen.
In every case of suspected battered baby syndrome
where there are no obvious rib fractures the whole
length of the rib should be carefully examined for
evidence of old injuries. The presence of multiple rib
fractures must be considered as having resulted from
non-accidental trauma, after the exclusion of such
causes as a vehicular accident or manual compression in
an attempt to revive a baby either by a doctor or by the
parent. Bone disease must also be excluded, but it
should be remembered that even a baby with a bone
disease can be battered or subjected to non-accidental
violence.

LONG BONE INJURIES.

A fracture of a long bone occurring as the only skeletal
injury in a case of suspected battering usually cannot be
distinguished from one resulting from such an accident
as falling from a cot but, when it occurs in conjunction
with a metaphysial injury or with multiple rib fractures,
it should be considered as a non-accidental injury,
unless there is definite proof to the contrary.
As in the case of the skeletal injuries already mentioned
the age of the injury and the mechanism by which it
was caused are important in establishing the diagnosis
and in cases where legal proceedings have been
instituted.
The type of fracture of a long bone sustained as a result
of falling from a cot or by being dropped can be spiral
or transverse. The spiral or oblique fracture occurs
when the baby falls with the limb under the body and
then rolls over so that a torsion force is applied (Fig.
3.53). The fracture may be transverse if the limb strikes
a hard projecting object during the fall. The spiral
fracture is more common than the transverse in cases
of accidental trauma.
In the battered baby syndrome the spiral fracture can
be caused by a torsion force applied to a limb as
when the baby is forcibly jerked upwards and rotated
while held by the wrist or ankle. A spiral fracture of the
humerus may result when the wrist is held (Fig. 3.54)
or a fracture of the femur when the baby is held by
the ankle. In the absence of any corroborative evidence
one cannot say how this type of fracture was caused,

but the presence of an associated metaphysial avulsion injury, as in the wrist (Fig. 3.55), is conclusive evidence of non-accidental trauma.

Fig. 3.53. Oblique fractures of the shaft of the right femur with no visible callus, indicating that the injury is less than a week old. This is the torsion-type fracture which could be caused by an accidental fall. The presence of metaphysial injuries with callus formation in the distal end of the left femur and in the proximal end of the left tibia indicate that the fractures of the right femur could be the result of a non-accidental injury. Judging by the amount of callus present, these metaphysial injuries are about 2 to 3 weeks old.

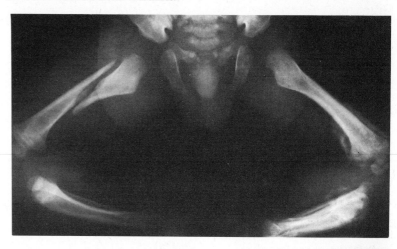

Fig. 3.54. Oblique or torsion-type of fracture of the distal aspect of the humerus. If this were the only skeletal injury present, one could not say whether this was the result of accidental or non-accidental trauma. Even when there are multiple injuries of other bones, apart from metaphysial lesions, as was the case in this infant, one can only surmise as to the mechanism.

Fig. 3.55. Torsion-type of fracture of distal aspect of shaft of humerus. Here there are metaphysial lesions of the distal ends of the radius and ulna with detached pieces of bone and periosteal new bone along the shaft of the ulna. In this case one can state with confidence that these injuries are due to non-accidental trauma. Without any history one can surmise that the infant was held by the wrist and forcibly jerked upwards and rotated, or that he was swung by the wrist. The mother later confessed to pulling the infant violently out of the cot by his wrist.

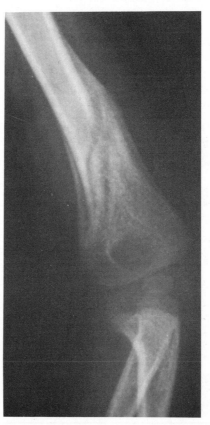

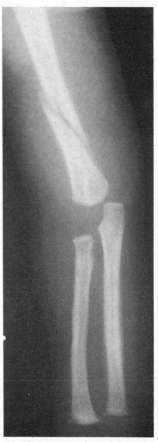

A transverse fracture in the battered baby syndrome is usually the result of a direct blow (Figs. 3.56, 3.57 and 3.58). It has occurred, however, as the result of an indirect injury where the mother, holding the baby by both wrists, jerked him forcibly out of the cot. This action caused a transverse fracture of the mid-third of the left ulna and a transverse fracture of the mid-third of the right radius (Fig. 3.59). Such bilateral fractures could rarely be caused by an accidental fall and the presence of an avulsion injury of the distal metaphysis of the right humerus confirmed that the fractures were the result of a non-accidental trauma. A similar mechanism could have produced the fractures shown in Fig. 3.60. These are transverse fractures of the proximal ends of both humeri. There are also present oblique fractures of the outer ends of the clavicles. All four fractures could have occurred at the same time and the most likely explanation is that the baby was held by the elbows and forcibly jerked upwards and forwards.

Avulsion of a muscle from its attachment to a long bone can result in the so-called traumatic myositis, which is ossification of a parosteal haematoma (Fig. 3.61).

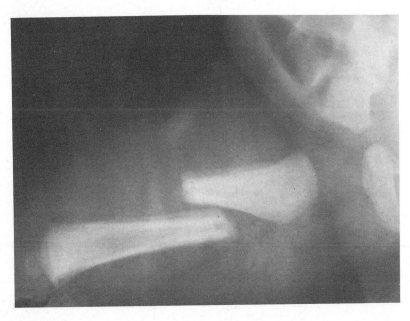

Fig. 3.56. Transverse facture of the femur caused by a direct blow with an iron bar.

Fig. 3.57. Transverse fractures resulting from direct injuries to the left 5th and right 1st metacarpals.

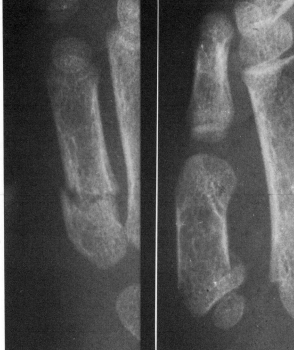

Fig. 3.58 (left). Transverse fracture of the shaft of the humerus resulting from a direct blow. This could also be caused by the infant falling with the arm underneath the body, but this is unusual in a normal bone. Transverse fractures can occur spontaneously or as the result of slight direct or indirect trauma when a bone lesion is present as in osteogenesis imperfecta (see Fig. 4.3) and in the porotic bones of spina bifida (see Fig. 4.23) and rickets.

Fig. 3.59 (right). Transverse fractures of the shafts of the right radius and left ulna resulting from indirect trauma. The mother stated that she took the baby by both wrists and jerked him upwards. The metaphysial lesion in the distal end of the right humerus is consistent with the mother's statement. It would be unusual for bilateral transverse fractures to be caused by a fall.

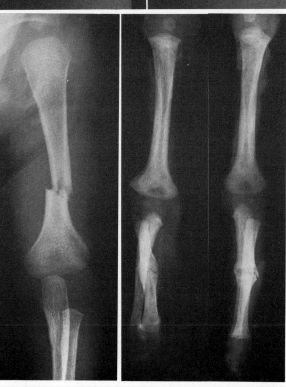

A

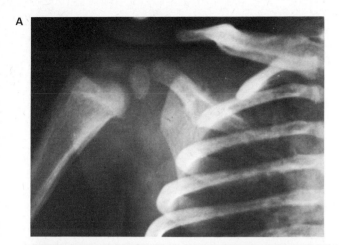

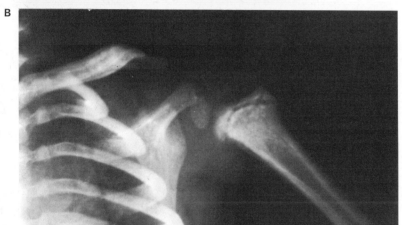

Fig. 3.60. Transverse fracture of the proximal end of the shaft of each humerus with an oblique fracture of the outer end of each clavicle. A possible explanation as to the cause is that the infant was held by the elbows and jerked violently upwards.
(a) Right shoulder.
(b) Left shoulder.

B

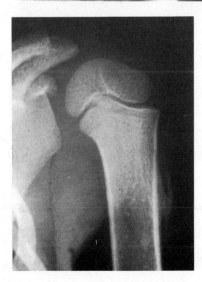

Fig. 3.61. Ossified subperiosteal haematoma on the shaft of the humerus resulting from an avulsion injury in a known case of an abused 3 year old girl. 8 months previously there was extensive swelling of the whole arm.

Estimation of the age of the injury.

As regards the estimation of the age of the fracture of a long bone, the same criteria apply as in the case of the metaphysial injury and the multiple rib fractures; that is, callus is not visible on a radiograph for seven to ten days following the injury and the subsequent estimation of the age becomes a matter of experience.

In the case of a fracture of the skull it is unusual for any noticeable healing change to take place for four to six weeks following the injury. The fracture may become more definite in the days following the injury, especially if a subdural haematoma develops.

Fracture of the spine.

A fracture of the spine may occur (Fig. 3.62) and, if it is an isolated lesion, it will not be diagnostic as it will not differ from that sustained by an accidental injury. If the fracture is associated with other skeletal injuries the diagnosis will probably be made on the presence of these injuries.

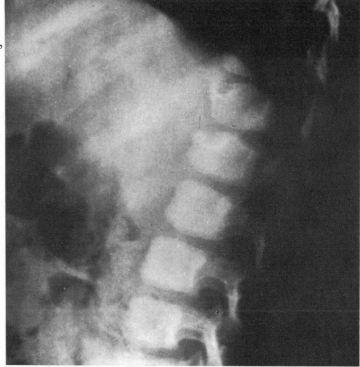

Fig. 3.62. Crush fractures of the anterior aspects of the bodies of thoracic 12 and lumbar1 in a boy aged 3 years, sustained by falling off a wall. Similar appearances have been described in battered babies by Swischuk (*Radiology*, **92**, 733, 1969).

4. Differential Diagnosis

There are several diseases where the bone injuries can simulate those seen in the battered baby syndrome but, in most of these, the clinical examination should establish the diagnosis. It is important, however, that the doctor should be conversant with these radiological appearances when examining a suspected case of the battered baby syndrome and when giving evidence in a court of law on such a case.

OSTEOGENESIS IMPERFECTA

In the majority of cases the diagnosis is not in doubt. In the neonatal type there are multiple fractures of tubular shaped long bones (Fig. 4.1) or multiple fractures where the bones are thin and bowed (Fig. 4.2). In less severe cases the bones may be thin and not fractured (Fig. 4.3). The cases that can simulate the battered baby syndrome are those where the bones appear normal at birth and fractures occur several months later, as in the following case. A female infant aged five months was re-admitted to hospital with a history of persistent vomiting following an operation for pyloric stenosis three months previous. Examination

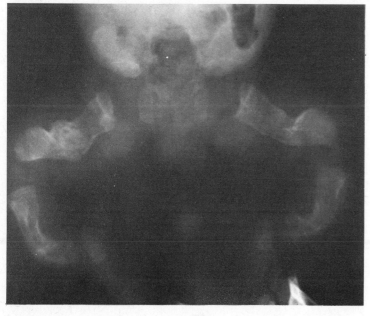

Fig. 4.1. Osteogenesis imperfecta—neonatal type with multiple fractures in tubular-shaped long bones.

51

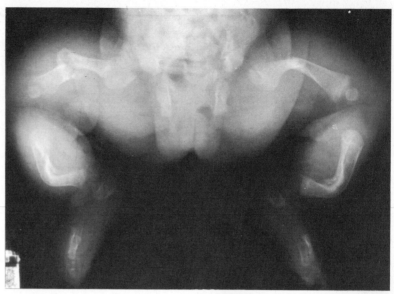

Fig. 4.2 (above).
Osteogenesis imperfecta—
neonatal type with multiple
fractures in thin and bowed
bones.

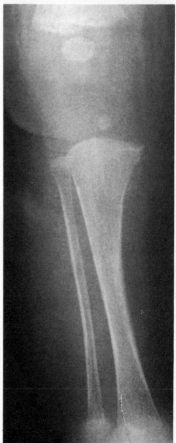

Fig. 4.3 (right). Osteogenesis
imperfecta—thin porotic
bones with no fractures.

of the bones which were included in radiographs of the chest and of barium meal examination showed no abnormality. Over the next three years during her stay in hospital she sustained numerous fractures of the ribs (Fig 4.4) and of the long bones (Figs. 4.5 and 4.6). Several years later the bones showed gross changes typical of osteogenesis imperfecta (Figs. 4.7 and 4.8). Had this infant not been in hospital when the fractures occurred there would have been a strong suspicion that this was a battered baby, especially with the posterior situation of the rib fractures, which is such a common feature in the battered baby syndrome.

It will be noted, however, that the fractures of the long bones involve the diaphyses and not the metaphyses, as occurs in the avulsion-type injury. These are not avulsion fractures, but fractures occurring in porotic bones, either spontaneously or as the result of slight trauma.

A similar type of fracture is to be seen in the porotic bones of a case of spina bifida (see Fig. 4.26). Although

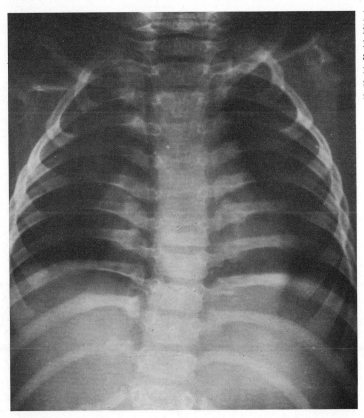

Fig. 4.4. Osteogenesis imperfecta—multiple fractures of the posterior aspects of the ribs indistinguishable from those seen in the battered baby syndrome.

Fig. 4.5. Osteogenesis imperfecta—fracture of the proximal aspect of the diaphysis of the left humerus, not involving the metaphysis.

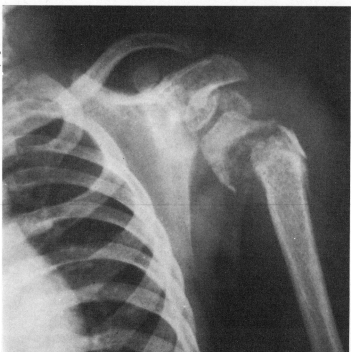

Fig. 4.6. Osteogenesis imperfecta—fractures of the diaphyses of the right femur, right tibia and left femur. The metaphyses are not involved. The fractures tend to be transverse: this is a common feature where the fracture is spontaneous. These fractures have occurred at different times.

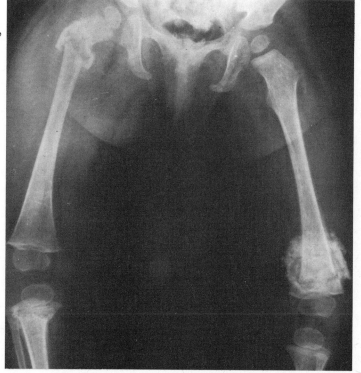

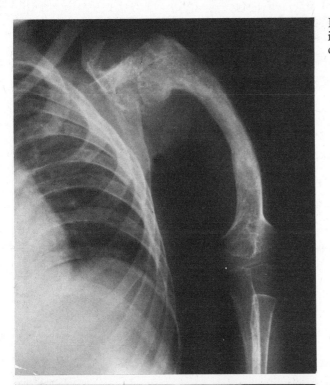

Fig. 4.7. Osteogenesis imperfecta—typical gross deformity in the humerus.

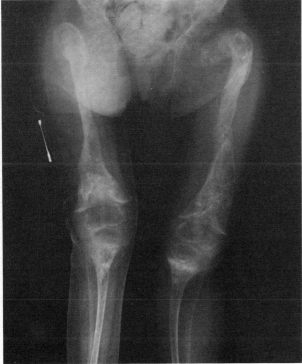

Fig. 4.8. Osteogensis imperfecta—the lower limbs of the same case as in Figure 4.7.

exuberant callus is said to be a feature of osteogenesis imperfecta (Fig. 4.9) it can occur around a fracture of a normal bone in a battered baby, especially if, as so often happens, the fragments are not immobilized (Fig. 4.10). Excessive new bone formation is not an uncommon feature following trauma to the distal end of the femur in a case of spina bifida (see Fig. 4.28) and it can occur in cases of osteomyelitis involving the metaphysis (see Fig. 4.23). There are, however, other features which are diagnostic of osteogenesis imperfecta, such as blue sclerotics and a mosaic pattern in the posterior aspect of the skull (Fig. 4.11). The possibility that skeletal injuries in a case of osteogenesis imperfecta may have resulted from non-accidental trauma should, however, not be overlooked.

Fig. 4.9 (left). Osteogenesis imperfecta—exuberant callus formation around the proximal aspect of the right femur, 6 weeks after the injury. Note that the callus at the distal end of the left femur (Fig. 4.3) has largely resolved in 3 weeks.
Fig. 4.10 (right). Exuberant callus in a battered baby where the fragments were not immobilised and where there was no bone disease.

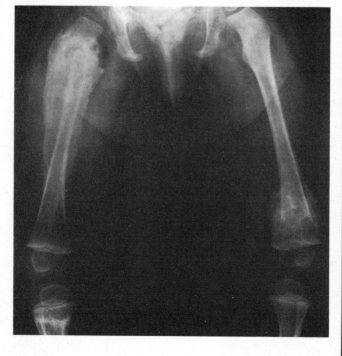
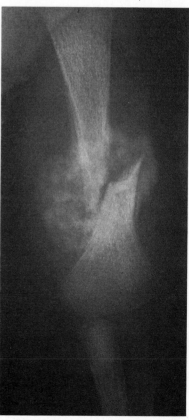

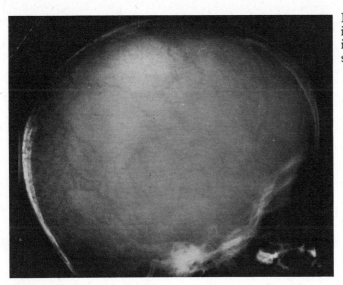

Fig. 4.11. Osteogenesis imperfecta—mosaic pattern in the posterior aspect of the skull.

SCURVY

The bone changes in scurvy with the fractured metaphysis and calcification in the subperiosteal haematoma closely resemble the appearances of a metaphysial lesion in the battered baby syndrome (Figs. 4.12 and 4.13). In scurvy, however, there is a generalised osteoporosis and the metaphyses of most of the long bones will be involved.

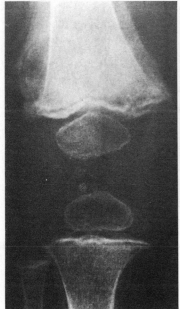
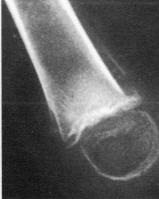

Fig. 4.12 (left). Scurvy—the distal end of the femur showing a fractured and separated metaphysis with calcification in the subperiosteal haematoma. Similar, but less extensive, changes are present in the tibia.

Fig. 4.13 (right). Scurvy—lateral view of the distal metaphysis of the femur showing a fractured metaphysis and early calcification in a subperiosteal haematoma. The appearances of these two cases resemble those resulting from avulsion injuries in a battered baby (see Figs. 3.17 and 3.27).

CONGENITAL SYPHILIS

In congenital syphilis there may be a fractured and separated metaphysis of a long bone with periosteal new bone along the shaft (Fig. 4.14). Extensive periosteal new bone is a common feature on the shafts of the limb bones and this tends to be symmetrical. It rarely extends to the metaphysis, though the bone adjacent to the metaphysis is often porotic (Fig. 4.15). The presence of an area of erosion on the medial aspect of the proximal end of tibia (Wimberger's sign) in association with the periosteal new bone formation is diagnostic of congenital syphilis (Fig. 4.16). There are no changes in the metaphysis as would be seen in the case of an avulsion injury. Occasionally, however, the metaphysial border may be eroded by the syphilitic inflammation and in such a case it may be difficult to exclude superimposed trauma (Fig. 4.17). The fact that the periosteal new bone can occur on several of the long bones of the limbs with no metaphysial damage should serve to distinguish congenital syphilis from the battered baby syndrome.

Fig. 4.14. Congenital syphilis—changes in the wrist of a neonate showing separation of the metaphyses of the distal ends of the radius and ulna with periosteal new bone extending along the shafts. Such a complete separation of a metaphysis is rarely seen in a battered baby; this would require great force in a normal bone and would be accompanied by more extensive new bone formation in a subperiosteal haematoma and probably in the adjacent soft tissues.

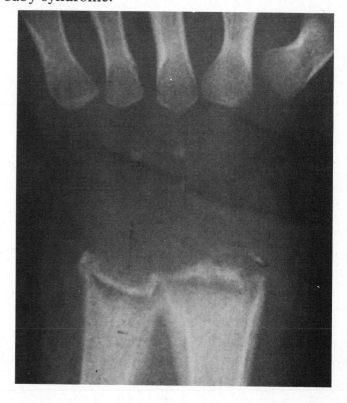

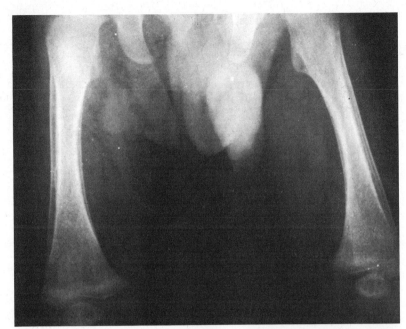

Fig. 4.15. Congenital syphilis—periosteal new bone on the shafts of both femora with porosis of the distal ends. There are no changes in the metaphyses to suggest injury. This periosteal new bone layer is more marked than what one would expect in the normal (see Fig. 3.31).

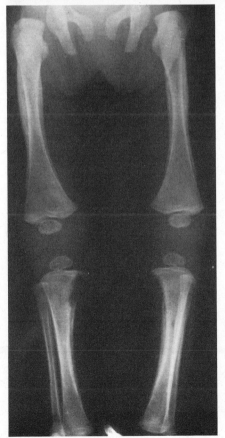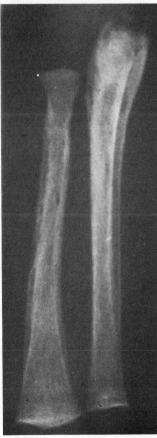

Fig. 4.16 (left). Congenital syphilis—erosion of the proximal end of the medial border of each tibia, Wimberger's sign.
This appearance is diagnostic of congenital syphilis and bears no resemblance to an avulsion injury. Periosteal new bone on the shafts of the femora and tibiae does not extend to the metaphyses. In the main the lesions in congenital syphilis tend to be symmetrical.

Fig. 4.17 (right). Congenital syphilis—periosteal new bone on the shafts of the radius and ulna with erosion of the olecranon and areas of erosion in the shaft of the radius. The new bone on the ulna extends to the metaphysis where there is extensive erosion and sclerosis. It would be difficult to exclude a superimposed traumatic lesion here.

INFANTILE CORTICAL HYPEROSTOSIS OF CAFFEY (Caffey's Disease)

In this condition periosteal new bone forms along the shafts of several long bones (Figs. 4.18 and 4.19). Where this new bone extends to the metaphyses, the case may resemble the periosteal new bone resulting from an avulsion injury, especially when the injury involves the proximal and distal metaphyses of a long bone (see Fig. 3.21). In Caffey's disease the metaphyses will show no evidence of injury. The clavicles may be involved (Fig. 4.20) and the resulting diffuse cortical thickening may resemble callus formation, especially if the fracture is longitudinal and bilateral (see Fig. 3.60). Usually, however, a fracture is either a short oblique one or transverse and the callus formation is more localized (Fig. 4.21). In a large proportion of cases of Caffey's disease, the mandible will show cortical thickening.

Fig. 4.18 (left). Caffey's disease—periosteal new bone formation along the shafts of the radius and ulna; this does not extend to the metaphyses, which are normal.

Fig. 4.19 (right). Caffey's disease—the tibia and fibula of the same case as in Figure 4.18.

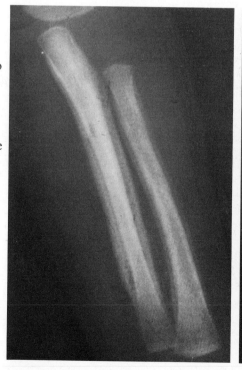
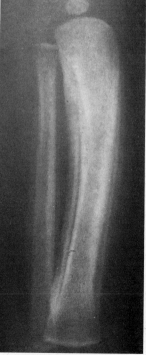

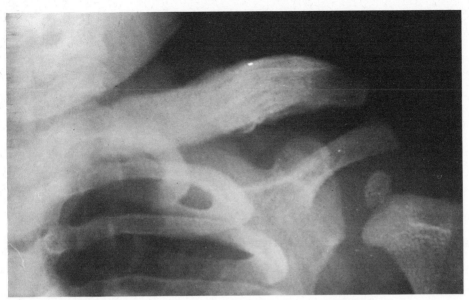

Fig. 4.20. Caffey's disease—involvement of the clavicle with layers of periosteal new bone resulting in a diffuse thickening. This may bear some resemblance to the callus formation associated with a longitudinal fracture (see Fig. 3.59).

Fig. 4.21. Fractures of both clavicles in the battered baby syndrome. The callus in this case is more localized around the fractures and does not resemble the diffuse thickening of Caffey's disease.

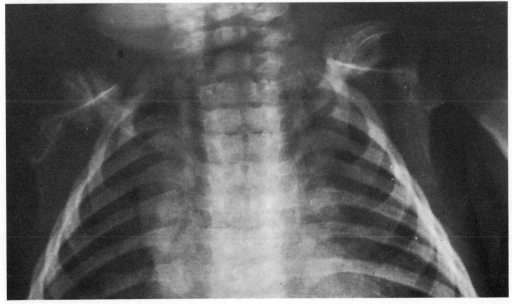

OSTEOMYELITIS

When the metaphysis of a long bone is affected by osteomyelitis, the appearances can resemble those of a metaphysial avulsion injury; the metaphysis may become irregular and periosteal new bone forms along the shaft (Fig. 4.22) and compare (Fig. 3.19c). In some cases there may be excessive calcification in the surrounding soft tissues resembling a severe avulsion injury (Fig. 4.23). The deformity resulting from osteomyelitis in the region of a metaphysis, with thickening of the cortex (Fig. 4.24). can simulate the thickened cortex of an old subperiosteal haematoma (see Fig. 5.7).

Periosteal new bone formation can occur when the inflammation is of the soft tissues and not of the bone, as in cellulitis (Fig. 4.25). There is no metaphysial damage and the soft tissue swelling would probably be more extensive than that resulting from a haematoma.

Fig. 4.22. Osteomyelitis involving the distal metaphysis of a femur. There are areas of erosion adjacent to the metaphysis and periosteal new bone is forming along the shaft, resembling the early appearances of a metaphysial avulsion injury (see Fig. 3.19c).

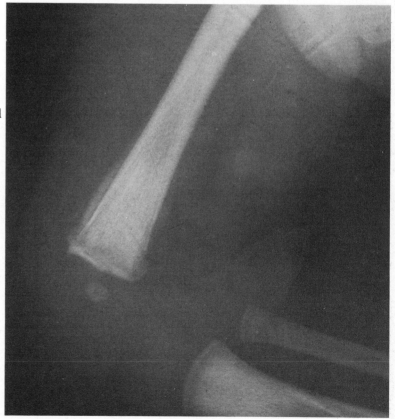

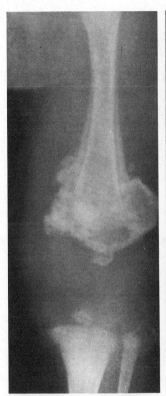
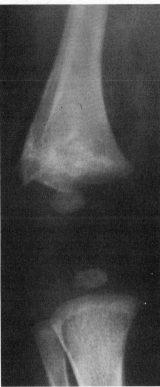

Fig. 4.23 (left). Osteomyelitis of distal end of a femur with extensive calcification in the surrounding soft tissues and with periosteal new bone formation on the shaft. These appearances simulate those caused by a severe metaphysial injury.

Fig. 4.24 (right). Osteomyelitis—deformity of the distal end of the femur resulting from osteomyelitis. This resembles the deformity following the resolution of a calcified subperiosteal haematoma due to an avulsion injury of the metaphysis (see Fig. 5.4).

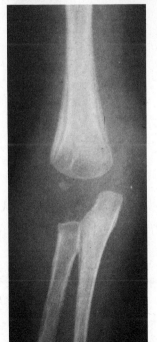

Fig. 4.25. Periosteal new bone on the humerus secondary to cellulitis around the elbow. There is no abnormality of the metaphysis to indicate an injury.

SPINA BIFIDA

In a case of spina bifida where the legs are paralysed and the bones are porotic very slight trauma can cause a fracture, which is usually transverse, of the distal end of the shaft of the femur (Fig. 4.26) or can cause a dislocation of the epiphysis with associated damage to the metaphysis (Fig. 4.27). These injuries are commonly accompanied by extensive haemorrhage and subsequent new bone formation in the adjacent soft tissues (Fig. 4.28); this creates an appearance not unlike that seen in a case of a battered baby, except that this degree of dislocation of the epiphysis is uncommon as a result of non-accidental injury (see Fig. 3.27).

As in osteogenesis imperfecta the fact that the slight trauma may be non-accidental should not be overlooked. It should also be remembered that the fractures in both these diseases can occur spontaneously.

Fig. 4.26 (left). Spina bifida—transverse fracture of the distal end of the shaft of the femur following slight trauma.

Fig. 4.27 (centre). Spina bifida—dislocation of the distal epiphysis of the femur following slight trauma. There is also a fracture of the proximal end of the tibia.

Fig. 4.28 (right). Spina bifida—extensive new bone formation in the adjacent soft tissues following a dislocation of the femoral epiphysis and damage to the metaphysis. It is unusual to find this degree of dislocation in the battered baby syndrome.

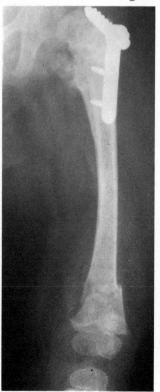
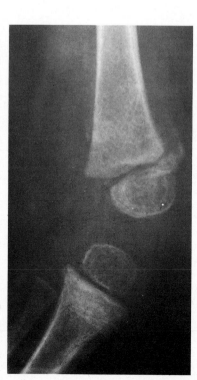
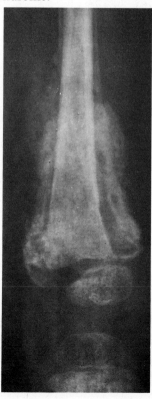

5. Illustrative and Problem Cases

The first three cases are described to illustrate the importance of not ignoring pieces of bone which are lying loose near a joint following an injury and which have the appearance of being detached from the metaphysis.

CASE 1

An eleven month old male child was taken to a casualty department by the father who said he had dropped the child and he thought the leg might be damaged. No obvious fracture was detected on clinical examination; flexion and extension of the right knee produced normal movements; no lateral movement was tested. One radiograph was taken of the pelvis and both lower limbs. The report stated that there was no fracture, but there was a piece of bone lying loose near the distal end of the right femur (Fig. 5.1). The father

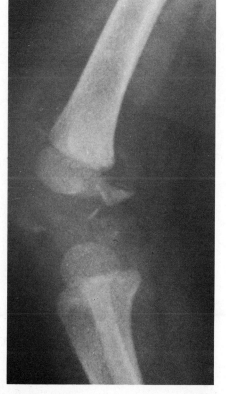

Fig. 5.1. Loose piece of bone lying by the distal end of the femur. It will be noticed that there is a dislocation of the tibiofibular joint.

was told to bring the child to the hospital on the following day if there was no improvement. That night the child sustained a fracture of the left femur and of the skull, from which he died soon after. A skeletal survey prior to autopsy showed a fracture dislocation of the right knee (Fig. 5.2 a and b) and a metaphysial lesion of the distal end of the left tibia (see Fig. 3.15). Both these injuries were estimated to be about a week old. There was a fracture of the left femur, not present on the previous day. The survey also revealed several ribs with old fractures in the posterior aspect (see Fig. 3.50). Had a skeletal survey been carried out in the first instance when a loose piece of bone was apparently the only evidence of injury, these other lesions would have been demonstrated and would have indicated that the child had sustained two previous non-accidental traumatic incidents.

Fig. 5.2a. A post-mortem film of the right knee shows the true extent of the dislocations, not only of the tibiofibular joint, but also of the distal femoral epiphysis and of the proximal epiphysis of the tibia. Early periosteal new bone formation on the femur indicates that the injury is about a week or more old. Great violence must have been used to produce so severe an injury; it could not have been caused by a fall.
Fig. 5.2b. Shows the knee joint bisected longitudinally at autopsy. (Figs. 3.15 and 3.50 show the other injuries revealed by a skeletal survey of this infant.)

A

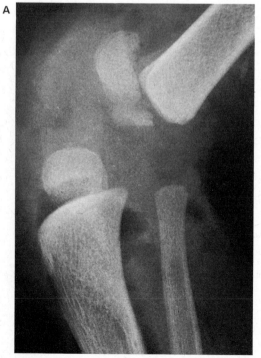

B

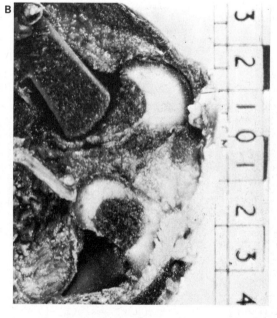

CASE 2

A male infant aged three and a half months was
admitted to hospital with a fracture of the parietal area
of the skull and diastasis of the sutures (Fig. 5.3).
Radiographic examination of the swollen left knee
showed pieces of bone detached from the metaphysis of
the distal end of the femur (Fig. 5.4). A history of a fall
was given by the parents but the presence of a
metaphysial lesion in the femur suggested that the
infant had been swung by the leg and that his head had
struck a hard object. Radiographic examination eighteen
days later showed marked new bone formation around
the distal half of the femoral shaft (Fig. 5.5) and an
increase in the degree of sutural diastasis (Fig. 5.6). The
child was seen again four months later when the femur
showed advanced remodelling (Fig. 5.7). He was
re-admitted to hospital five months after the original
injury with another fracture of the left femur (Fig. 5.8).
This was another case of the battered baby syndrome
occurring several years ago when the significance of the
avulsion injury of the metaphysis was not fully
appreciated.

Fig. 5.3 (left). Fracture of the parietal bones with diastasis of the sutures.
Fig. 5.4 (right). Fragments of bone detached from the distal metaphysis of the left femur.

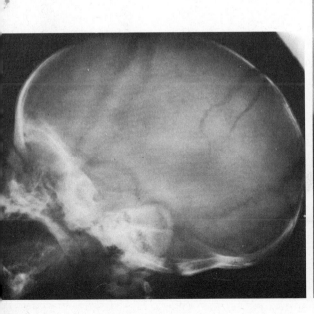
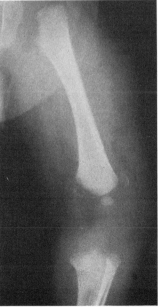

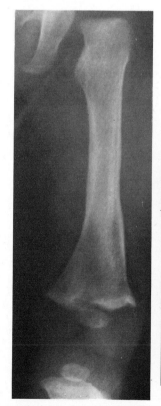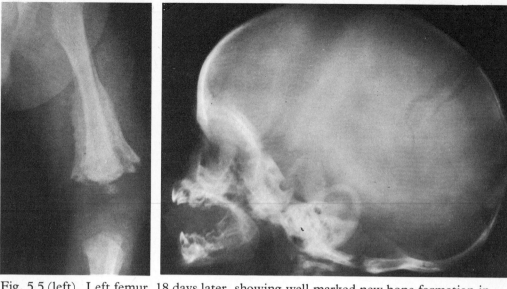

Fig. 5.5 (left). Left femur, 18 days later, showing well marked new bone formation in the subperiosteal haematoma.
Fig. 5.6 (right). Skull, 18 days later, showing further sutural diastasis and a wider separation of the edges of the fracture.

Fig. 5.7 (left). Left femur showing well advanced remodelling 4 months after the first x-ray examination. A similar appearance can be seen in the remodelling following osteomyelitis (see Fig. 4.21).

Fig. 5.8 (right). Left femur; a transverse fracture 5 months after the initial injury, probably resulting from direct trauma.

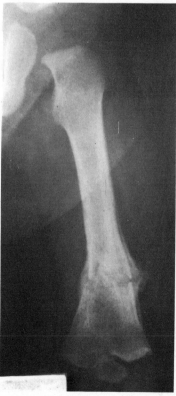

CASE 3

A female infant aged six weeks was brought to hospital by the mother with a history that, with the infant in her arms, she had fallen off the bed and subsequently the infant's right elbow became swollen. On radiographic examination a small piece of bone was seen apparently detached from the distal end of the humerus (Fig. 5.9). A week later, following another fall, the infant was admitted to hospital with a head injury, when a fracture of the skull was confirmed radiologically. A further radiograph of the right elbow showed periosteal new bone formation along the shaft of the humerus (Fig. 5.10). This appeared to be more than a week old, indicating that the injury was several days old at the time of the first visit to hospital. The radiographic

Fig. 5.9 (left). Right elbow with a small fragment of bone detached from the distal end of the humerus.

Fig. 5.10 (right). Right elbow, one week later than shown in Figure 5.9, with periosteal new bone along the shaft of the humerus. The amount of new bone indicated that the injury is more than a week old.

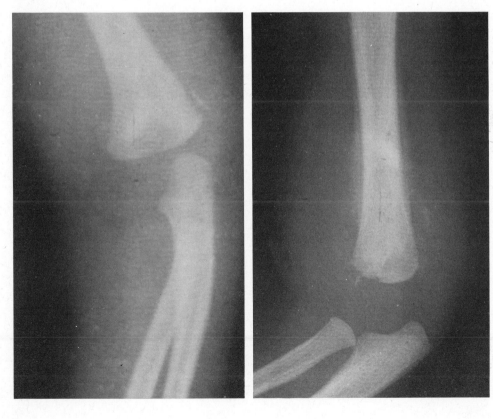

examination also revealed a fracture of the mid-shaft of the right femur and a dislocation of the left hip (Fig. 5.11). The fracture of the skull could have occurred at the time of the second fall but, judging by the amount of callus present, the fracture of the right femur and the dislocation of the left hip could have resulted from the first fall and could have been present at the first visit to hospital. If the mother's story were true, the piece of bone detached from the right humerus could have resulted from such a fall and, on radiological evidence alone, a skeletal survey would not have been justified. If, however, there was any doubt concerning the veracity of the story, then a non-accidental avulsion injury would have had to be considered and a skeletal survey carried out.

In this case, this would have revealed the other injuries at the first examination and the infant would not have been subjected to the second traumatic incident.

Fig. 5.11. Fracture of the mid-third of the shaft of the right femur with callus formation. Dislocation of the left hip with calcification in the adjacent soft tissues. The estimated date of these injuries is between 1 and 2 weeks.

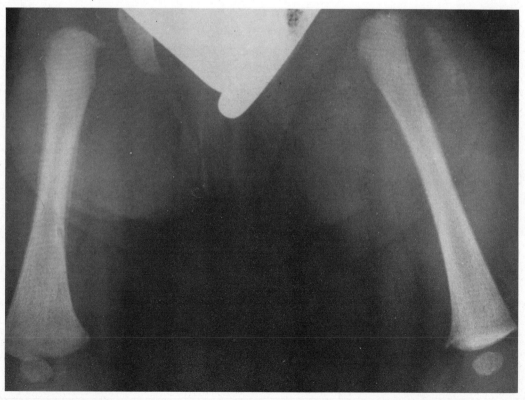

CASE 4

The following case exhibits unusual injuries to a
forearm and stomach.
A male infant was born three weeks premature with a
birth weight of 5 pounds 4 ounces and, as a result,
stayed in hospital for eight days following delivery.
At two months of age he was admitted to hospital with
intermittent vomiting and, on examination, he was
found to be undernourished with multiple areas of old
and recent brusing all over the body, particularly over
the buttocks and the right side of the face and lips,
together with the right side of the chest. This latter area
in particular was tender to touch. Radiographs taken at
that time revealed fractures of the necks of the fifth to
the seventh ribs inclusively of approximately four weeks
duration, with a suggestion of fractures of the necks of
the fifth and sixth left ribs. In addition there was an
unusual transverse fracture of the upper end of the shaft
of the right ulna (Fig. 5.12). This injury was considered
to be approximately one week old, and suggested that it
had been caused as a result of direct violence applied by
or against the forearm.
Fundal examination at this time was negative.
Following admission the child commenced to thrive and
feed normally and rapidly put on weight. At the time of
admission, at the age of three months, he weighed 9
3 ounces and when discharged home four weeks later
13 pounds 7 ounces, at which time all the fractures
had healed satisfactorily. The child was referred to the
social services department who accepted responsibility
for supervising the child and when seen a month after
discharge from hospital weighed 14 pounds 12 ounces.
The child died at the age of six months i.e., two months
after discharge from hospital. His weight then was 14
pounds.
At autopsy there was no evidence of natural disease that
could have caused or contributed to death at that
particular moment in time. There was the classical tear
of the upper lip and an abrasion beneath the point of
the chin (Fig. 5.13), in addition to multiple areas of
bruising. On internal examination there was a split
laceration of the front wall of the stomach with deep
bruising of the under surface of the right lobe of the
diaphragm. On opening the stomach there were
multiple submucosal split tears across the stomach. The

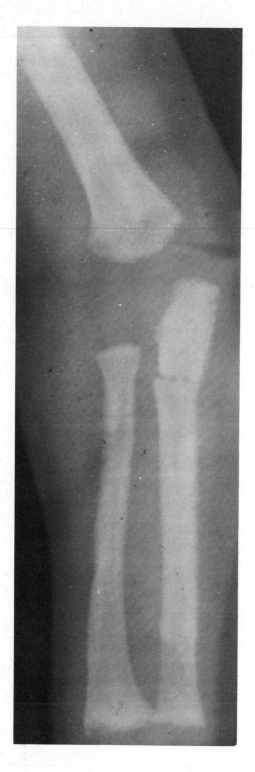

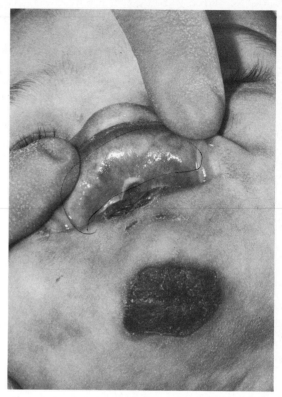

Fig. 5.13. Photograph showing classical tear of the upper lip and an abrasion beneath the point of the chin.

Fig. 5.12. Radiograph showing unusual transverse fracture of the upper end of the shaft of the right ulna.

opinion expressed was that these injuries could only have been caused by direct violence applied by or against a lax abdomen which resulted in subsequent rupture and generalised peritonitis with spillage of the stomach contents into the abdominal cavity. The resulting reaction on the organs, particularly the liver, was consistent with being of approximately forty-eight hours duration prior to death. Radiographic examination after death and subsequent radiographs of the rib cage after autopsy revealed multiple fractures of the ribs. All these fractures appeared to have occurred at or about the same time and were consistent with having been produced approximately two to three weeks prior to death. The fractures previously noted on radiographic examination showed evidence of healing and no deformity, as one would have anticipated, there being no evidence of any bone disease to make the skeleton more brittle or more susceptible to such fractures. Although one felt that the forearm injury was a result of direct violence, in view of its unusual appearance, it was felt that in giving evidence one could not exclude the possibility of it having been caused by other means. In retrospect, however, it is now felt that there could not have been another explanation other than that of direct violence.

CASE 5

Late development of infantile coxa vara following non-accidental violence is suggested in this case. A boy age 3 years was admitted to hospital complaining of pain in the left hip and inability to walk following a fall. Radiographic examination showed a fracture of the neck of the left femur with coxa vara and fragments of bone in the adjacent soft tissues. (Fig. 5.14). This lesion was not of recent origin. The boy was a known victim of battering at the age of two months when he sustained metaphysial injuries of the proximal end of the left humerus (Fig. 5.15) and of the distal end of the left tibia (Fig. 5.16). The radiographs showed no injury of the left hip and unfortuately follow-up radiographs were not taken. There was no history of injury, disability or pain until the recent injury nearly 3 years later.
Blockey (1969) described a case of a battered baby aged 5 months who sustained a metaphysial injury of the

distal end of the femur and no demonstrable injury of
the hip. Two years later the child was found to have a
fracture of the neck of the femur and 5 years after the
battering, radiographs revealed an infantile coxa vara.
Blockey suggested that a fissure fracture of the femoral
neck occurred at the time of the battering and that
separation and shearing were later brought about by
weight bearing. Fairbank (1948) states that a fissure
fracture of the neck of the femur, a diagnostic
prerequisite of infantile coxa vara, is distinct from the
epiphysial line. A distinction is thus made between
infantile coxa vara and congenital coxa vara. McDougall
(1961) describes cases where the untreated fracture of
the femoral neck in childhood results in infantile coxa
vara. In the case here described it is suggested that
the avulsion injury of the distal metaphysis of the tibia
was caused by swinging the baby by the ankle and that
by this action a fissure fracture of the femoral neck was
sustained, with later development of infantile coxa vara.

Fig. 5.14. Infantile coxa vara
with fracture of the neck of
the left femur showing partial
absorption and increased
density; the capital epiphysis
is porotic and there are
fragments of new bone in the
soft tissues. These changes
indicate that the lesion is not
of recent origin.

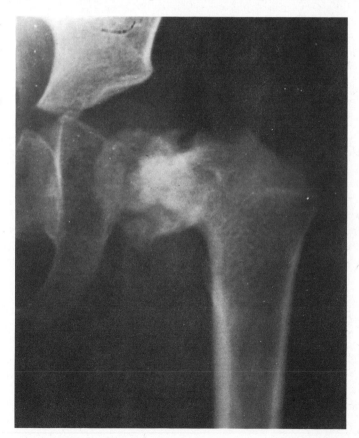

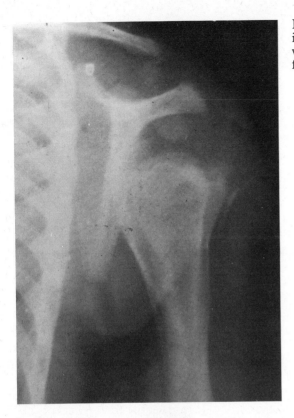

Fig. 5.15. Metaphysial injury of the left humerus with periosteal new bone formation.

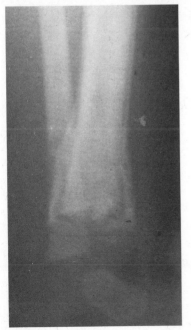

Fig. 5.16. Metaphysial injury of the tibia showing the bucket-handle appearance.

CASE 6

A male baby aged 6 weeks was admitted to hospital with pneumonia. Radiographic examination showed a staphylococcal pneumonia of the right lung with an associated empyema. The radiographs also revealed numerous fractures of the posterior aspects of the left ribs and fractures of the costochondral junctions on both sides. The estimated age of these fractures was from 2 to 3 weeks. In addition there were dislocations of the costovertebral articulations, 5 to 12 on the right side, with fractures of the 7th and 12th ribs; this injury appeared to be of recent origin (Fig. 5.17). Soon after admission the baby developed osteomyelitis of the left tibia and of the right index finger. Six weeks following the estimated date of the original trauma, osteomyelitis became evident in the posterior aspects of the left lower ribs at the sites of the fractures and in several of the right ribs adjacent to the dislocations (Fig. 5.18). The empyema was drained; the condition of the baby deteriorated and after several cardiac arrests he died. At autopsy bilateral paravertebral abscesses were found and the osteomyelitis of the ribs was confirmed. There was no evidence of osteomyelitis of the fractured costochondral junctions or of the fractured left ribs above the limit of the paravertebral abscesses (Fig. 5.19). This baby was the victim of an assualt which caused the fractures of the ribs. In the radiographs taken 2 to 3 weeks after this assualt there was no evidence of osteomyelitis or of any disease of these ribs, so that the violence required to produce these injuries must have been severe. To produce the dislocations of the costovertebral articulations great force would be required which would certainly fracture the ribs; in this case, however, there were only two slight fractures. It must therefore be assumed that the ligaments of these articulations were rendered lax by infection, so that slight trauma only would be necessary to cause the dislocations. This was taken into consideration at the trial of the father for manslaughter.
It is unusual in a case of empyema for the ribs to become infected and even more rare for the contralateral ribs to be involved, so that it can be argued that had these ribs not been injured they would not have become infected. The bilateral paravertebral abscesses could have resulted from infected haematomata caused by the

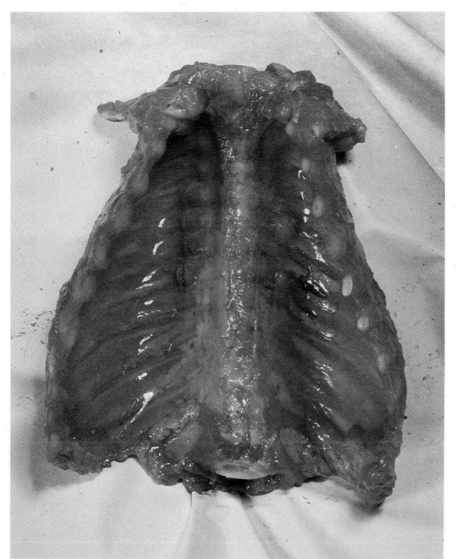

Fig. 5.19. Post-mortem specimen which shows the extent of the osteomyelitis of the right middle and left lower ribs. The previous well formed callus in the posterior aspects of the left lower ribs has been eroded. The upper fractured left ribs and the fractured costochondral junctions on both sides show no evidence of osteomyelitis.

trauma; if they had been secondary to a staphylococcal
septicaemia one would have expected all the fractured
ribs to be infected, but not one costochondral junction
was involved.
How much, therefore, did the battering contribute to
the cause of death? The father pleaded guilty to
manslaughter and was given probation for 3 years.

Fig. 5.17 (left). Fractures of the left ribs 4 to 11 in the posterior aspects and of the left
costochondral junctions 5 to 7. The estimated age of these injuries is from 2 to 3 weeks.
There are dislocations of the right costovertebral articulations 5 to 11 with a fracture of
the neck of the 7th rib only. There is a right sided empyema.

Fig. 5.18 (right). Radiograph taken 6 weeks after the estimated date of the original
trauma. There are early changes due to osteomyelitis in the right middle and left lower
ribs. The right sided empyema has not cleared.

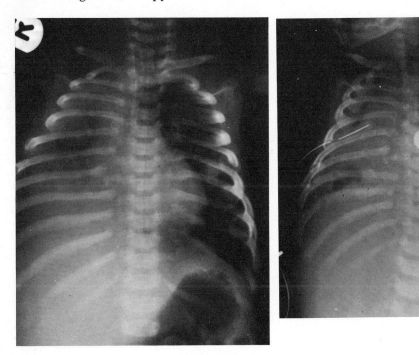

REFERENCES.

Blockey, N. J. (1969) *Journal of Bone and Joint Surgery*, **51-B**, 106.
Fairbank, H. A. T. (1928) *Infantile or Cervical Coxa Vara*, Robert
Jones Birthday Volume, a collection of surgical essays, p.225.
Oxford University Press.
McDougall, A. (1961) *Journal of Bone and Joint Surgery*, **43-B**, 16.

6. The Eye of the Battered Infant

Alan S. Mushin

Evidence of ophthalmic manifestations in the battered baby syndrome has been steadily accumulating in recent years. The occurrence of sub-hyaloid haemorrhages in association with subdural haematoma has long been established, but it is now clear that many battered infants sustain ocular damage of other sorts, and this may be extensive. Every child suspected of having suffered physical abuse should undergo full ophthalmic examination, including fundus examination under anaesthesia if necessary.

OCULAR SIGNS IN BATTERED-CHILD SYNDROME:

Bruising around the eye. (Lids: periorbital bruising)

Most children sustain a 'black eye' at some time in their lives, but any child who appears with two black eyes, especially if there is evidence of bruising elsewhere, should be regarded with suspicion. (Fig. 6.1). It is remarkable that these periorbital haematomata are only very rarely associated with other ocular damage. They heal rapidly, without sequelae. There are many in whom the bruising subsides before they reach an ophthalmologist.

Conjunctival and sub-conjunctival haemorrhages

These are not common, and heal rapidly. (Fig. 6.2). They may occur,
(a) associated with periorbital bruising, or
(b) associated with fractures of the anterior cranial fossa.

Anterior segment injuries

(a) Hyphaema has been seen in battered infants, and is an indication of very severe direct trauma to the eye.
(b) Traumatic mydriasis has been described, but the pupillary dilatation has not been permanent.
(c) Subluxation of the lens has also been described (Fig. 6.3); it is not easy to break the zonular fibres in a child, and lens subluxation indicates that considerable trauma

78

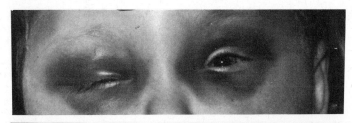

Fig. 6.1. Bruising around the eyes—note that both sides are involved.

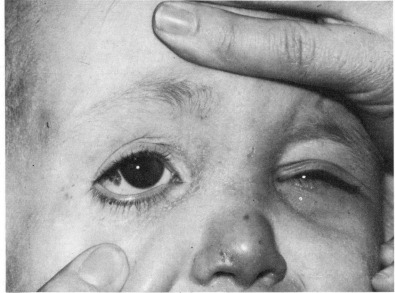

Fig. 6.2. Subjunctival haemorrhage in a battered infant.

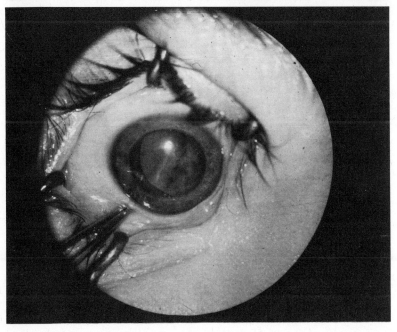

Fig. 6.3. Subluxation of the lens due to trauma (note the pigment dispersal on the detached retina behind the lens).

has occurred, sufficient to cause associated intraocular haemorrhage, or retinal detachment.

Retinal detachment

This is a rare condition in childhood and infancy, and in this age group is due either to trauma, severe intraocular disease, or heredo-congenital retinal disease. Any infant with a retinal detachment should be regarded as having sustained severe ocular trauma, and investigated for evidence of further trauma elsewhere. The case shown had a total retinal detachment (Fig. 6.4a), and a small area of choroido-retinal scarring in the retinal periphery of the *other* eye. These peripheral atrophic scars, (Fig. 6.4b.) particularly in the lower temporal quadrant of the fundus, have been found in some 30 reported cases of battered infants, all of whom were referred for ophthalmic examination after the diagnosis of physical abuse had been made.

Intraocular haemorrhage (Figs. 6.5 and 6.6)

Retinal, pre-retinal (sub-hyaloid) and vitreous haemorrhages are commonly encounted in children who have sustained trauma to the head, especially in association with subdural haematoma. The haemorrhages may be scattered through the retina, and there may also be haemorrhage into, and swelling of, the optic disc (i.e. papilloedema). The vast majority of these haemorrhages absorb completely over a period of four to twenty weeks, leaving no sequalae and no residual visual deficit. But if haemorrhage is severe permanent damage may occur due to:

(a) Organisation and fibrosis in the retina itself, leading to macular scarring and loss of central vision.
(b) Breaking through of the haemorrhage into the vitreous. When vitreous haemorrhage occurs, the outlook for vision is much more doubtful; at best there is a small degree of retinal fibrosis, and at worst the organising and contracting scar may lead to a traction retinal detachment. This may also be the mechanism of the peripheral retinal scarring which is sometimes encountered in a battered infant, and of some cases of Coats' disease (a rare retinopathy of childhood).

L.E.

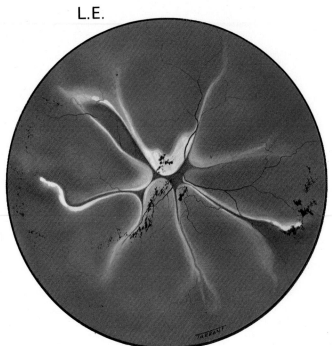

Fig. 6.4a. Total retinal
detachment in a child of 2
who had other evidence of
physical abuse (evidence of
healed long bone fractures).

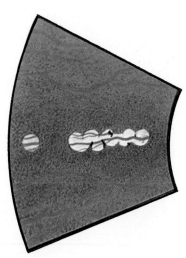

Fig. 6.4b. Peripheral
atrophic retinal scar in an
otherwise normal eye in an
infant suspected of having
been abused on more than
one occasion.

PERIPHERY R.E.

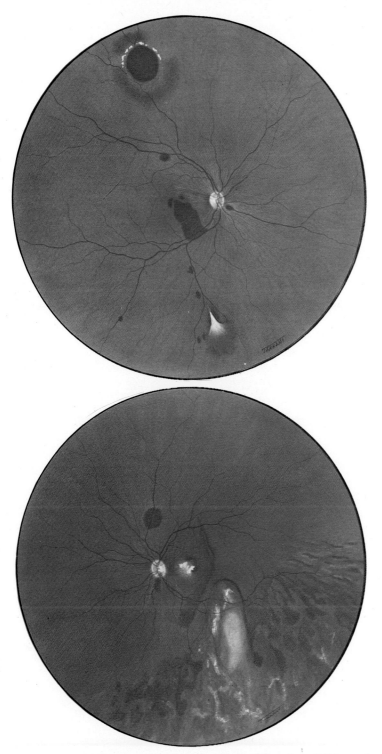

Figs. 6.5 and 6.6. Right and left eyes of a Nigerian child age 2 who was admitted to hospital with 'failure to thrive'; she had evidence of long bone fractures. The plates show in the right eye, evidence of haemorrhage of different ages (the haemorrhage at the top has signs of cholesterol around, it, suggesting that it is some weeks old, while the central haemorrhage is fresh), and in the left eye, very extensive haemorrhage in the retina and vitreous, with a macular scar and a choroidal rupture. The final outcome in this child was that the right eye has normal vision, but the left vision is severely depressed.

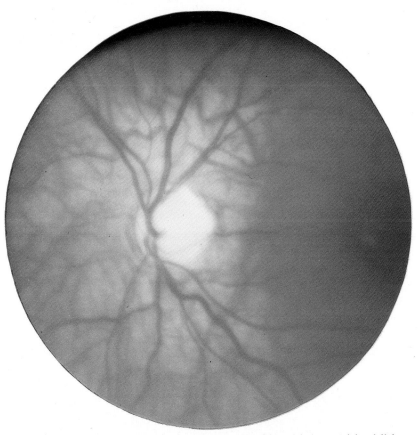

Fig. 6.7. Optic atrophy as a late result of head injury (this child had a subdural haematoma associated with bruising and rib fractures at 18 months of age. At the time he had retinal haemorrhages, which resolved; but unilateral optic atrophy associated with squint was the final result.

Optic Atrophy

As a late sequel of injury, optic atrophy may develop (Fig. 6.7). It is usually due to intracerebral injury but in rare cases follows severe intraocular damage. Optic atrophy and macular scarring have been seen in the same eye.

Damage to the visual pathways and the visual cortex is the commonest cause of permanent visual impairment in battered infants, and several cases have been reported in which cortical blindness has been the main residual handicap when all other injuries have healed. In these patients there is always evidence of intracranial haemorrhage but ophthalmic examination may be completely normal.

Squint

Any eye which does not see well may 'turn' and the presence of a squint in an infant suspected of having been physically abused demands careful fundus examination. The likely findings are macular damage or optic atrophy. Not only may this be important in establishing the diagnosis but clearly conventional orthoptic treatment is of no use if the squinting eye is structurally damaged. (This late and permanent squint is quite different from the transient paralytic squint which frequently occurs when there is rise in the intracranial pressure due to subdural haematoma).

REFERENCES and SUPPLEMENTARY READING.

Aron, J. J., Marx, P., Blanck, M. F., Duval, R., and Luce, R. (1970) *Ann. Ocultist*, **203**, 533.

Friendly, D. S. (1971) *Trans. Amer. Acad. Ophthalmol. Otolaryngol.*, **75**, 318.

Gilkes, M. J., and Mann, T. P. (1967) Lancet, 2:468.

Harcourt, R. B., and Hopkins, D. (1973) Ophthalmic aspects of the battered child syndrome. In *Neuro-ophthalmology*, Vol. 7, p. 87, ed. Smith, J. L. St. Louis: C. V. Mosby.

Harcourt, R. B., and Hopkins, D. (1971) *Brit. Med. J.*, **3**, 398.

Hollenhorst, R. W., and Stein, R. A. (1958) *Arch. Ophthalmol.*, **60**, 187.

Jensen, A. D., Smith, R. E., and Olson, M. I. (1971) *J. Paediatr. Ophthalmol.*, **8**, 270.

Kiffney, G. T., Jun. (1964) *Arch. Ophthalmol.*, **72**, 231.

Maroteaux, P., Fessard, C., Aron, J. J., and Lamy, M. (1967) *Presse Med.*, **75**, 711.

Mushin, A. S. (1971) *Brit. Med. J.*, **3**, 402.

Mushin, A. S., and Morgan, G. (1971) *Brit. J. Ophthalmol.*, **55**, 343.

Walsh, B. B., and Hoyt, W. F. (1969) Clinical Neuro-ophthalmology, 3 ed., p. 234. Baltimore: Williams & Wilkins.

7. Prevention and Treatment

If you have experience of caring for 'crying children' under five, you would have been distressed for the parents as well as for the infant. Nearly every week there are Press reports of cruelty to children by their parents or guardians resulting in either irreparable brain or eye damage, skeletal trauma or death.

As soon as non-accidental injury is suspected by the family doctor, casualty officer, health visitor or social worker, the child should always be admitted to hospital for study and for safety. If not already involved the family doctor and health visitor should be notified, so that they may discuss any information in their possession (Cooper, 1970). The paediatrician, radiologist and medico-legalist should call in other colleagues, such as a neurosurgeon, when appropriate. He should also discuss the findings with the parents (Cooper, 1970), who occasionally will admit part of the true story, especially if they see the paediatrician as someone who will help rather than accuse or condemn.

Obviously no one wants to split up families if it can be avoided. One solution, after careful assessment, may be to return the child to his home and parents, making certain that they have adequate support and treatment (Antice, 1968) from the medical and nursing profession, the children's department, the National Society of Prevention of Cruelty to Children, and other social services.

In serious cases criminal proceedings against the parent(s) are taken for the appropriate offence. Provided that a conviction is secured, disposal is a matter for the court acting upon the available evidence. There should, however, be concern for the discrepancy from one case to another, one court to another, and one part of the country to another.

The battered child syndrome, a clinical condition in infants who have received serious physical abuse, is a frequent and apparently increasing cause of sudden death in young children. It is a problem of increasing importance, calling for the full co-operation of the medical, social and legal authorities in this country. There is a definite lack in medical education concerning ill-treatment in children: according to some authorities less than a third (i.e. 20 per cent) of such cases seen by doctors are reported to the authorities.

There seems little doubt that the present situation shows an explosive increase of a certain type of traumatic clinical picture. The extent of the explosion is underlined by the fact that until quite recently it was not included in the punch diagnosis records of the most important children's hospital in the country. There can be little doubt that, in the early stages of the escalation, it was missed by clinicians and unacceptable both to magistrates and judges, because of the emotional rejection of violence being inflicted upon babies by adults associated with them in the home. Although the findings are quite variable, the syndrome should be considered in any child exhibiting evidence of possible trauma or neglect (fractures in various stages of resolution, subdural haematoma, multiple soft tissue injuries including laceration of the mouth, poor skin hygiene, or unexplained malnutrition) or where there is a marked discrepancy between the clinical findings and the past history as supplied by the parents. In all such cases, the doctor should have a low threshold of suspicion and have a radiographic study of the whole skeleton. In this way the presence or absence of the characteristic multiple bony lesions in various stages of healing can be ascertained. A negative x-ray does not exclude the diagnosis, the basis of which depends upon the nature and recurrence of injuries, the time taken to seek medical advice, and a discerpant history. Psychiatric knowledge pertaining to the problem is relatively meagre (Helfer and Kempe, 1968) and the type and degree of physical attack varies greatly. Parents who inflict such abuse on their offspring do not necessarily have psychopathic or sociopathic personalities, or come from one particular social class more than another. In a number of cases there is some defect in parental character structure present, while not infrequently the infant is the product of an unwanted pregnancy, a pregnancy which began before marriage, or at some other time felt to be extremely inconvenient. Regardless of the doctor's personal reluctance to become involved in such cases, he should remember that his moral obligation is to the child and he should be aware that at least 60 per cent of these children are liable to further injuries, or death, if not fully investigated. Complete investigation, including a full radiographic study, therefore, is necessary for the child's protection, together with steps to prevent repetition of the ill-treatment through normal medical channels social services and, in extreme cases, by legal sanctions. Clearly the general practitioner, casualty officer and paediatrician have a clear responsibility both to the child and his family as a total unit. In dealing with the abused, maltreated or battered child, the general practitioner has one of his most difficult roles to play, for he may find himself emotionally involved. In such an event, he should immediately refer the case to another less involved, possibly at a distance, particularly if it is a small town or comminity.

Although the safety of the child must be the primary consideration one must remember that battering parents need help, and, above all, a good relationship with a helping person, priority in many cases for rehousing, day nursery placement, and even temporary reception of the children into care during periods of stress and crisis. To assist in preventing family break-down, local authorities were given powers and duties under the Children and Young Persons Act, 1963, to provide advice, guidance and assistance including material aid to promote the welfare of children and diminish the need to receive them into care. This legislation provides an effective instrument for preventing or mitigating child neglect, while abuse calls for attention to psychological stresses rather than to material needs. It has been suggested (Gibbens and Walker, 1956) that child guidance treatment may be necessary to help parents understand a child's behaviour. Close co-operation between doctors and social agencies is essential at all stages. Mutual respect for the duties, responsibilities and professional practices of the several disciplines involved in the management of the battered child and his family is an important aspect of the problem which will be solved only by the achieving of a greater understanding of its underlying causation. If this succeeds, there will be less cause for the almost hysterical demand for legislation to introduce obligatory reporting of cases when a child is found to be injured—accidents can happen. The most exciting and encouraging aspect of this problem must lie in the area of prevention. We must try to devise reliable means of identifying parents who demonstrate a potential for child abuse. Such parents could then be given help and support in order to prevent a further battered baby.

REFERENCES

Antice, E. (1968) *World Medicine*, **4**, 50.
Cooper, C. E. (1970) *J. od Med. Women's Fed.*, **52**, 93.
Gibbens, T. C. N., and Walker, A. (1956) Cruel Parents. London: Inst. for the Study and Treatment of Delinquency.
Helfer, R. E., and Kempe, C. H. (1968) *The Battered Child*. Univ. of Chicago Press.

Index

Printed by T. & A. Constable Ltd., Edinburgh